P9-DNG-273

COUNTRY COOKIES

Also by Lisa Yockelson

THE EFFICIENT EPICURE
GLORIOUS GIFTS FROM YOUR KITCHEN
COUNTRY PIES
COUNTRY CAKES

COUNTRY COOKIES

---◆◆◆---

AN OLD-FASHIONED COLLECTION

Lisa Yockelson

ILLUSTRATIONS BY WENDY WHEELER

1817

HARPER & ROW, PUBLISHERS, New York
Grand Rapids, Philadelphia, St. Louis, San Francisco
London, Singapore, Sydney, Tokyo, Toronto

COUNTRY COOKIES. Copyright © 1990 by Lisa Yockelson. All rights reserved. Printed in the United States of America. No part of this book may be used or reproduced in any manner whatsoever without written permission except in the case of brief quotations embodied in critical articles and reviews. For information address Harper & Row, Publishers, Inc., 10 East 53rd Street, New York, N.Y. 10022.

FIRST EDITION

Library of Congress Cataloging-in-Publication Data

Yockelson, Lisa
   Country cookies: an old-fashioned collection/Lisa Yockelson.—1st ed.
     p. cm.
   Includes index.
   ISBN 0-06-016258-9
   1. Cookies. I. Title.
TX772.Y63   1990
641.8'654—dc20   89-46131

90 91 92 93 94 DT/RRD 10 9 8 7 6 5 4 3 2 1

For Susan Lescher,

with admiration

Contents

————◆◆◆————

Acknowledgments

It has been a wondrous experience to have compiled so many of the recipes I know and love into a trilogy of baking books entitled *Country Pies, Country Cakes* and *Country Cookies.* In writing these small primers, I have been forced sometimes to look backward—through the old recipes my mother and grandmother passed down to me, and to sift through all the other recipes that I have worked out over the years and made part of my baking tradition.

Even though these books are a personal trip through one author's baking kitchen, I know that good cooks from all over this country share similar feelings about what makes a good recipe. Many thanks to all of my readers who, with lots of kind and encouraging words, keep me going.

For their advice and creativity, friendship and humor, I wish to thank the following people:

To Susan Friedland, my editor at Harper & Row, for her commitment to making *Country Cookies* just the right finish to this series of baking books, her perseverance and dedication to the art of recipe writing; and to Nicholas Noyes, assistant to Susan Friedland, for his ability to handle all the details of this book's production with ease and grace.

To Susan Lescher, my literary agent, for her support of this three-book project, her understanding and fellowship; and to Carolyn Larson, assistant to Susan Lescher, who gives out doses of reassurance when needed.

To Joseph Montebello, Creative Director at Harper & Row, for his keen vision as to how these baking books should look.

To Wendy Wheeler, illustrator of *Country Pies, Country Cakes* and *Country Cookies,* for her marvelous interior drawings and covers, which add such an appealing visual dimension to whatever I write.

To Bob Kelleter, Food Editor of *The Washington Post,* for his good cheer.

To Linda Greider, food writer and editor, for her encouragement and professional friendship.

To Phyllis Richman, syndicated columnist and food critic for *The Washington Post,* for always sharing ideas, thoughts and theories about food and recipes.

To Lisa Ekus and Lisa Shanahan at the Lisa Ekus Public Relations Company, for their resourcefulness and dedication to cookbooks.

To Ann Amernick, talented pastry chef and cookbook author, for sharing her insights into the baking process.

To Steven the Bear, who can sniff out oatmeal-raisin cookies (hold the raisins, please) baking miles away from home, for his compassion and affection.

And again, to Grandma Lilly, who taught me how to bake.

THE JOY OF COUNTRY COOKIES

A heap of Sugar Cookie Hearts piled high in a basket lined with a gingham cloth, Cinnamon–Cashew "Dunking" Cookies tucked into an old enameled cookie box, a batch of crunchy Ginger Crisps or Heavenly Hash Brownies layered on a Depression-glass plate, several dozen Oatmeal–Raisin Saucers nestled in an earthenware batter bowl—these are country cookies, sweet morsels that are homey and good to eat.

Like pie and cake baking, cookie making is an established specialty of the American kitchen. While the soup pot simmered away on a corner of the stovetop, old-time cooks would stir together a mound of cookie dough; in between chores, they'd pinch off gobs, arrange them on sheet pans in neat rows and bake the cookies in shifts. Later, lucky family members and friends would raid the cookie jar and munch away.

The old-fashioned cookies in this book taste of pure and familiar ingredients. They are made up of such things as oatmeal, nuts, dried and fresh fruit, aromatic spices, buttermilk, molasses, coconut and chocolate. These goodies are perfect for filling up big glass apothecary jars or shiny metal cookie tins.

There are fat, cakelike cookies that, once upon a time, you would have found at the corner bakery or cooling on racks in your grandmother's kitchen. And there are hand-crafted cookies that are just waiting to become part of your holiday tradition. These are the cookies that I love to bake—the meltingly rich rolled cookies made with butter and plenty of vanilla, soft molasses drops or fudgy chocolate morsels—and they seem to recapture all the textures and flavors we remember from childhood.

Just like *Country Pies* and *Country Cakes, Country Cookies* is meant to be your companion in the kitchen, to guide you—sometimes nostalgically—through the ways of baking drop cookies by the generous dozens, making square or bar cookies from thick batters and stamping out layers of dough with fanciful cutters.

GOOD AND FRESH:
NOTES FROM A
COOKIE KITCHEN

Wendy Wheeler

When I was growing up, my mother always mixed up a batch of cookie dough in an enormous crockery bowl with a wooden spoon—even though an electric mixer stood ready and waiting to do the job on a countertop nearby. Step by step, she'd blend together the ingredients, then drop spoonfuls of dough onto lightly buttered and floured sheets; she'd shove the pans into the oven (sometimes mother was a "hurry up" kind of baker) and remove them when golden, firm to the touch and just right.

It must be true—a plate of warm cookies, made from many wholesome things, creates memories that linger on and on.

THE COUNTRY CUPBOARD

There's nothing quite like the sight and scent of fresh cookies moving from spatula to cooling rack, and the process for making them is simple and rewarding. Homemade cookies have a distinctively rich flavor and "crumb"; they are made from ingredients we use in everyday baking.

In my kitchen, I keep a "cookie larder"—a few shelves in the cupboard that hold all the baking essentials. (The cookie larder has many of the same ingredients used for making pies and cakes.) One shelf holds both all-purpose and cake flour, stored in large wide-mouth jars, and sugar (granulated, superfine, soft brown sugar, confectioners' and the flavored sugars I love to make). On another shelf, I arrange extracts (vanilla, chocolate, almond, lemon, coconut, maple), cornstarch, narrow tubes of plump vanilla beans, leaveners (baking powder, baking soda), dried fruit (raisins, figs, dates, apricots, peaches, pears, currants), oatmeal (plus homemade granola), cans of shortening and a range of chocolate (bittersweet bars, unsweetened squares, chocolate chips).

In the refrigerator I stockpile fresh butter and eggs, buttermilk and whole milk, sour cream, and containers of both light and heavy cream. The cookies in this book are made with extra-large eggs and fresh, not previously frozen, unsalted butter. Dairy ingredients should be brought to room temperature before adding them to cookie batters and doughs so that they blend in easily with the other ingredients.

Cookie Dough Enhancements

Using flavored granulated or confectioners' sugar is a favorite way of mine to strengthen the taste of many cookie doughs. Air-dried lemon peel or several split vanilla beans can be added to a jar of sugar, stored for a while to mellow, then used when mixing up a bowlful of dough.

Each sugar is easy to make and lovely to have on hand. Here's the method for both:

For Vanilla-Scented Granulated Sugar or Vanilla-Scented Confectioners' Sugar, place 3 pounds of granulated or confectioners' sugar in a large glass jar. Split 3 vanilla beans lengthwise with a sharp paring knife, keeping the beans intact but exposing the tiny seeds; bury the split beans in the sugar. Cover the jar with the lid. Store the sugar in a cool, dark place for at least 1 week before using.

For Lemon-Scented Confectioners' Sugar, remove 16 strips of peel from 2 large lemons using a swivel-bladed peeler. Place the strips on a sheet of wax paper and let them air-dry for about 12 to 24 hours, or until they are leathery. Turn the strips from time to time. Place 2 pounds of confectioners' sugar in a large clean jar. Bury the dried lemon strips in the sugar. Cover the jar with the lid. Store the sugar in a cool, dark place for at least 1 week before using. Use the sugar without the peels.

FROM PANTRY TO OVEN

Most of the cookies in this book are made in a free-standing electric mixer according to the following method: Butter or shortening (or a combination of both) is creamed until soft and malleable for 2 to 3 minutes. Sugar is added to the butter and the two are mixed together at moderate speed until fluffy. Eggs or egg yolks (or some of each) are beaten in, followed by flavorings, any liquid, fruit puree or melted chocolate (if used) and a flour mixture (which generally contains leavening and some spices). Assorted ingredients, such as chocolate or butterscotch chips, diced fruit, chopped nuts or marshmallow cream may be folded into the dough at the last moment.

Other cookies are made by combining melted butter (or melted butter and chocolate) in a bowl with sugar, eggs, flavoring and flour, using a wooden spoon or spatula. And a few of the bar cookies are made in two layers—the bottom layer consisting of a creamed cookie dough covered by a top layer of fruit, nuts, sugar, eggs and flavorings stirred together in a bowl.

A soft drop-cookie dough is formed into teaspoon- or tablespoon-size mounds (as specified in each recipe) and arranged on buttered and floured cookie sheets or on sheets lined with cooking parchment paper. Batterlike doughs for brownies and some bar cookies are spooned directly into baking pans; these bars or squares emerge from the oven baked as a solid "cake." The "cake" is then cut into small pieces when it reaches room temperature. (I refer to each pan of uncut brownies, bars, squares and so on as a "cake" because it describes what you will be working with.)

Yet another kind of cookie dough, which is firm enough to press into a decorative pan, is baked into huge nibbling cookies. This is the kind of dough used in the recipe for Giant Double Chocolate Rounds on page 96. The rounds are baked in fluted tart pans and are handy to serve at picnics or at casual suppers.

To make a batch of cookies, all you really need is a great big bowl, a long wooden spoon and some heavy cookie sheets, nothing more than what good cooks have been using for years.

An electric mixer, though, does make fast work out of creaming and blending ingredients, and is indispensable for making large quantities of cookie dough, a real time-saver if you are baking for a function, holiday sweet table or a cookie swap. But any of the doughs in this book may be made by hand, with excellent results.

Country cookies are usually baked on heavy aluminum cookie sheets; bar cookies, brownies or squares are baked in standard baking pans. My cookie sheets measure about 14 x 18 inches; the long sides are flat and the short sides have slight rims. Cookies baked on these sheets emerge from the oven evenly baked and with a delicate crumb.

If you are outfitting your cookie kitchen with these sheets, buy three or four of them. While one batch of cookies is baking, you can assemble the next; when the just-baked cookies are removed from the sheets onto racks, cool those sheets before placing more mounds of dough on them. Rotating the sheets in this fashion and cooling them in between baking also works well when you use sheets of parchment paper: Lay out the sheets on the countertop and space the mounds or cut-out shapes of dough on them, as directed in each recipe. Just before baking (or as soon as the sheets have cooled), carefully slide the parchment onto the sheets.

Usually, I line the sheets with cooking parchment paper, which is available in twenty-square-foot rolls at cookware and hardware stores and at some supermarkets. Buttering and flouring the sheets is a time-honored ritual for some, but I think cookies baked on ungreased parchment are far easier to slip off with a spatula. (The paper can be wiped clean with a damp cloth and used over again for your next cookie-baking session.)

Rolled cookie dough, which is generally sensitive to heat, should be cut out into shapes when the dough is well chilled; if you are working with thoroughly chilled rolled dough (such as the dough for my Sugar Cookie Hearts on page 84), stamp out cookies from one sheet of dough at a time. And unless your kitchen is very, very hot, drop cookie dough can stand at room temperature while you are working with it.

The cookies, ready to be sent into the oven, must be baked with care. I prefer to bake one tray of cookies at a time on the middle-level rack of the oven. If you are in a hurry, you can bake the cookies on the upper and lower third-level racks, but be sure to switch the sheets from top to bottom and front to back halfway through the baking time.

Brownies and other bar cookies are baked in 8-, 9-, or 10-inch square baking pans, a 13 x 9 x 2-inch rectangular baking pan or a 15 x 10 x 1-inch jelly roll pan. For these sizes, I prefer to use heavy aluminum; my favorite pans have straight sides, which lets you cut the cookies into neat bars or squares. Cookies baked in aluminum turn out even textured, with a good crumb.

The batter for my Cinnamon–Cashew "Dunking" Cookies (page 102), Chocolate Chip Rusks (page 106) and Layered Ginger Rusks (page 126) gets baked in empty aluminum ice cube trays. In the trays, the batter bakes into a small loaf that cuts into perfect rectangular slices; these trays work better than anything else. Thankfully, metal ice cube trays are still available at hardware stores. The trays come in two finishes, smooth and textured. I prefer the smooth-surfaced trays because the batter is less likely to stick to the surface when baked.

As you may know from reading *Country Pies* and *Country Cakes,* I love to shop at flea markets, tag sales and antique shows. At them, I add such things to my collection of cooking equipment as old pie tins, baking molds for corn bread and other batter breads, cookie plaques and cookie cutters. Over the years, I have found such lovely—and sometimes odd-shaped—cookie cutters as ornate angels, gingerbread ladies, fussy Victorian hearts, a man in the moon and even cutters in the shape of a muffin or loaf of bread. These are fun to collect and are a fine addition to your own heritage of baking equipment.

Keeping a full cookie jar is a tradition I heartily recommend—it seems that everyone loves to come home to a plate of fresh cookies. And I hope that the recipes in this volume encourage and preserve the art of cookie baking.

ON COOKIE
BASKETS

Wendy Wheeler

My favorite cookie basket is made out of clear Depression glass; it has a fluted rim and tall handle. Small cabbage roses are impressed around the base. When the basket is filled with Sugar Cookie Hearts or Fruit Clusters, it seems the essence of country—comforting, casual and charming.

Cookies look appealing layered in all kinds of baskets, whether they are made out of spindly twigs or wooden slats, porcelain or colored glass. Depending upon the depth of the basket, you can line it with several lacy paper doilies or a bright checkered tea towel just before adding the cookies. If the basket has a handle, it can be fussied up with a raffia bow tied to one side; or you can tie a small stack of cinnamon sticks with satin ribbon and attach that to the side of the basket.

Little packages of cookies look pretty arranged in a basket. Tie up handfuls of cookies in squares of cellophane, to resemble small pouches. Set the pouches in a basket that has been lined with curly Spanish moss. (For this, choose among the Vanilla Melt-a-Ways on page 32, Lemon Butter Balls on page 58, Sugar Cookie Hearts on page 84, Double Vanilla "Dog Bones" on page 54, Maple Bars on page 52 or Milk Chocolate–Almond Bars on page 100.)

Lots of miniature baskets, lined with moss and filled with single packages of cookies, are wonderful for handing out to dinner party guests or to children during the holiday season. And a huge basket filled with a still life of assorted cookies is a handsome addition to the Thanksgiving groaning board; be sure to include turkey-shaped sugar cookies made from the dough used in the recipe for Sugar Cookie Hearts (page 84).

HEART TO HEART

Heart-shaped baking implements—from cookie molds, to cutters, to individual cookie tins—are especially pleasing to use in the making of country cookies.

Over the years, I've amassed a whole range of these culinary implements, and I use them frequently in baking and as tabletop accessories. Old-time bakeware, such as small cutters and tiny molds, can be used to decorate teatime trays, or they can be tied to the sides of cookie baskets. Cookies look beautiful arranged in old heart-shaped wooden bowls or baskets, lined with a linen cloth. Heart-shaped trays made of porcelain, if you can find them, are ideal for serving tender rolled cookies or bar cookies; the trays have deeply scalloped edges and come in a variety of colors.

Heart-shaped cookie cutters come in many sizes, from the tiny one-inchers to the large five-inchers. There are several cookie doughs in this book that, once rolled out, are especially suited to stamping out with a heart-shaped cutter (these doughs must hold their shape while baking): the vanilla-rich dough in the recipe for Double Vanilla "Dog Bones" (page 54), the buttery chocolate dough on page 96 in the recipe for Giant Double Chocolate Rounds (omit the chocolate chips and bake the smaller cookies at 325 degrees for 20 minutes, or until firm) and, of course, the sugar cookie dough in the recipe for Sugar Cookie Hearts on page 84.

Soft, moldable doughs, such as the kind used for Vanilla Melt-a-Ways on page 32, Black Walnut Butter Drops on page 94 or Lemon Butter Balls on page 58 can be pressed into tin cookie plaques. The plaques look like madeleine molds, only each depression is in the shape of a heart. To fill these plaques, film the inside of each form with nonstick cookware spray, then gently press about a tablespoon of dough into each form (more or less according to size); gently smooth over the top with a flexible palette knife. After the cookies have been baked, invert them into cooling racks and dust with granulated or confectioners' sugar (if you are using the Vanilla Melt-a-Way dough, omit the final rolling in sugar; sprinkle the cookies with the sugar while they are warm).

COOKIE JAR
TREATS

COOKIE JAR TREATS

—◆◆◆—

*I*t's the little things that count: pints of homemade cranberry-pear butter lining the shelves of the kitchen pantry, a bottle of fresh raspberry syrup tucked into the refrigerator, a huge jar of cookies sitting on the kitchen counter. These are the small pleasures of life, and they are so nice to have around.

The cookie jar of my childhood was made out of pressed glass and its sweet contents were protected by a ground glass lid that kept the contents fresh and appealing. More than likely, you'd find my mother's famous Layered Ginger Rusks in the jar, or Oatmeal–Raisin Saucers. I could never resist any of those cookies, and I ate them a handful at a time. Between baking days, when the inside of the cookie jar was reduced to crumbs, mother would fill the jar with caramels. Caramels were never a satisfactory substitute for cookies, and this was a sad state of affairs.

To me, the sight of a full cookie jar evokes feelings of comfort and contentment. So I always keep my mother's big glass jar stuffed with cookies, varying the flavor and texture from week to week—to continue the nostalgic tradition and to have something good and sweet on hand.

In this chapter, you'll find soft applesauce cookies filled with raisins, oatmeal cookies flecked with bits of chopped pears and pecans and chewy chocolate cookies dotted with pools of chopped bittersweet chocolate. Once baked, these cookies are very hard to resist, and they just beg for a pitcher of ice-cold milk or a pot of hot coffee for serving alongside a basket of them.

Other cookies in this book that would fill up the cookie jar handsomely are my Double Vanilla "Dog Bones" (page 54), Ginger Crisps (page 78), Apple Butter Cookies (page 80), Pumpkin–Spice Cookies (page 89), Sugar Cookie Hearts (page 84), Black Walnut Butter Drops (page 94), Cinnamon–Cashew "Dunking" Cookies (page 102), Chocolate Chip Rusks (page 106), Fruit Clusters (page 120), Butterscotch–Granola Discs (page 122) or Banana–Oatmeal Pillows (page 114).

❖❖❖❖❖❖❖❖❖❖❖❖❖❖❖❖

Vanilla Melt-a-Ways

3¼ cups *unsifted* all-purpose flour

1 cup plus 3 tablespoons *unsifted* cake flour

1 teaspoon baking soda

¼ teaspoon baking powder

1 teaspoon cream of tartar

1 teaspoon salt

¾ teaspoon freshly grated nutmeg

These feather-light cookies, dotted with the seed scrapings from a plump vanilla bean, are tender and crisp—the combination of oil and butter makes them so. The cookie dough, which is uncommonly easy to work with, can be shaped into plump mounds, crescents or logs. Rolled in vanilla-scented sugar and baked until just golden, these sweet morsels are delicious served with a bowl of poached fruit or ice cream, or simply on their own, washed down with big cups of Hot Spiced Cider (page 133).

———❖❖❖———

Lightly butter and flour 4 cookie sheets, or line the sheets with lengths of cooking parchment paper; set aside. Preheat the oven to 375 degrees.

½ pound (2 sticks) unsalted butter, softened at room temperature

1 cup vegetable oil

1 cup *unsifted* Vanilla-Scented Granulated Sugar (page 19)

1 cup *unsifted* Vanilla-Scented Confectioners' Sugar (page 19)

Seed scrapings from the inside of 1 vanilla bean

1 extra-large egg, at room temperature

2 extra-large egg yolks, at room temperature

2 teaspoons pure vanilla extract

2 teaspoons milk, at room temperature

FOR ROLLING THE COOKIES:

About 1½ cups Vanilla-Scented Granulated Sugar (page 19)

About 60 cookies.

Sift the all-purpose flour, cake flour, baking soda, baking powder, cream of tartar, salt and nutmeg onto a sheet of wax paper.

Cream the butter in the large bowl of an electric mixer on moderate speed for 2 minutes. Add the oil and beat for 2 minutes. Blend in the granulated sugar and beat for 2 minutes. Add the confectioners' sugar and beat for 2 minutes. Blend in the vanilla bean scrapings, egg, egg yolks, vanilla extract and milk; beat 2 minutes, scraping down the sides of the mixing bowl frequently. On low speed (or by hand), blend in the sifted dry ingredients in 3 additions, beating just until the particles of flour have been absorbed.

Form balls, crescents or logs from level tablespoons of dough and carefully roll them in the granulated sugar. Place the cookies 1½ inches apart on the prepared cookie sheets. If you have formed the dough into balls, flatten each ball with the tines of a fork, making a criss-cross pattern.

Bake the cookies, one sheet at a time, on the middle-level rack of the oven for 10 to 12 minutes, or until pale golden and firm to the touch.

Transfer the cookies to cooling racks, using a wide spatula. Cool for 20 minutes. Store the cookies in an airtight tin.

Sour Cream–
Spice Cookies

2 cups *sifted* all-purpose
flour

1 cup plus 2 tablespoons
sifted cake flour

¾ teaspoon baking
powder

¾ teaspoon baking soda

¾ teaspoon salt

2 teaspoons ground
cinnamon

1 teaspoon freshly
grated nutmeg

1 teaspoon ground
ginger

½ teaspoon ground
allspice

¼ teaspoon ground
cloves

12 tablespoons
(1½ sticks) unsalted
butter, softened at
room temperature

¼ cup shortening

1 cup Vanilla-Scented
Granulated Sugar
(page 19)

These are dreamy cookies, rich in sour cream and eggs, and touched by five different spices. The cinnamon, nutmeg, ginger, allspice and cloves form a gentle backdrop to the dairy ingredients. I love them plain, but sometimes fancy them up with drizzles of confectioners' sugar glaze (see Baking Note).

A batch of Sour Cream–Spice Cookies is a perfect companion for a big earthenware bowl filled with Hot Spiced Cider (page 133).

————— ❖❖❖ —————

Lightly butter and flour 4 cookie sheets, or line the sheets with lengths of cooking parchment paper; set aside. Preheat the oven to 375 degrees.

Resift the all-purpose flour and cake flour with the baking powder, baking soda, salt, cinnamon, nutmeg, ginger, allspice and cloves onto a sheet of wax paper.

Cream the butter and shortening in the large bowl of an electric mixer on moderate speed for 2 minutes. Add the granulated sugar in 2 additions, beating for 1 minute after each portion is added. Add the light brown sugar and beat for 1 minute. Blend in the egg and egg yolks; beat 1 minute. On low speed (or by hand), blend in half of the sifted mixture. Blend in all of the sour cream, then the remaining sifted mixture.

Drop the dough by level tablespoons onto the prepared cookie sheets, placing the mounds 2 inches apart.

⅓ cup (firmly packed)
light brown sugar

1 extra-large egg, at
room temperature

2 extra-large egg yolks,
at room temperature

1 cup sour cream
blended with
2 teaspoons pure
vanilla extract

About 42 cookies

Bake the cookies, one sheet at a time, on the middle-level rack of the oven for 11 to 12 minutes, or until light brown and firm to the touch.

Transfer the cookies to cooling racks, using a wide spatula. Cool for 20 minutes. Store the cookies in an airtight tin.

Baking Note: To make the Confectioners' Sugar Glaze for this cookie, combine 3 tablespoons light cream, ¼ teaspoon pure vanilla extract and about ¾ cup confectioners' sugar. The glaze should be smooth and fluid enough to pour from a spoon (if not, stir in a teaspoon of sugar at a time if it is too thin, or several drops of milk if it is too thick). Drizzle the glaze over each cookie from a small spoon and let it firm up completely before storing the cookies between sheets of wax paper.

Orange–Raisin Drops

2½ cups *unsifted* all-purpose flour

½ cup *unsifted* cake flour

¾ teaspoon baking soda

¼ teaspoon baking powder

¾ teaspoon salt

½ teaspoon ground cinnamon

½ teaspoon freshly grated nutmeg

¼ teaspoon ground allspice

¼ teaspoon ground ginger

8 tablespoons (1 stick) unsalted butter, softened at room temperature

½ cup shortening

1 cup maple sugar

½ cup granulated sugar

3 tablespoons freshly grated orange rind

2 teaspoons pure orange extract

The tangy flavor of freshly grated orange rind and orange juice winds through this cookie dough, partnering nicely with the golden raisins, maple sugar and spices. Soft, old-fashioned Orange–Raisin Drops are particularly good teamed up with tall glasses of milk or mugs of hot chocolate, and they are a welcome addition to the school (or office) brown bag lunch.

My paternal grandmother, Lilly Yockelson, and I used to bake these cookies together on many an afternoon. Grandma loved golden raisins and used them here, along with a cupful of chopped dates. I like the cookies without the dates, and I have made the dough a bit more delicate by replacing a small amount of the all-purpose flour with cake flour.

❖❖❖

Lightly butter and flour 4 cookie sheets, or line the sheets with lengths of cooking parchment paper; set aside. Preheat the oven to 375 degrees.

Sift the all-purpose flour, cake flour, baking soda, baking powder, salt, cinnamon, nutmeg, allspice and ginger onto a sheet of wax paper. Cream the butter and shortening in the large bowl of an electric mixer on moderate speed for 2 minutes. Add the maple sugar and beat for 2 minutes. Add the granulated sugar and beat for 1 minute longer. Beat in the orange peel and orange extract. Blend in the eggs, one at a time, beating well after each addition. Beat in the egg

2 extra-large eggs, at
  room temperature
2 extra-large egg yolks,
  at room temperature
¼ cup freshly squeezed
  orange juice
1¾ cups golden raisins

About 48 cookies

yolks. Blend in the orange juice. On low speed (or by hand), blend in the sifted dry ingredients in 2 additions, beating just until the particles of flour have been absorbed. By hand, stir in the raisins.

Drop the dough by rounded tablespoons onto the prepared cookie sheets, placing the mounds 2 inches apart.

Bake the cookies, one sheet at a time, on the middle-level rack of the oven for 12 to 14 minutes, or until light brown and just firm to the touch.

Transfer the cookies to cooling racks, using a wide spatula. Cool for 20 minutes. Store the cookies in an airtight tin.

Chocolate Gems

2 cups *sifted* cake flour

1 cup *sifted* all-purpose flour

¾ teaspoon baking powder

¾ teaspoon baking soda

1 teaspoon salt

½ teaspoon ground cinnamon

12 tablespoons (1½ sticks) unsalted butter, softened at room temperature

1 cup Vanilla-Scented Granulated Sugar (page 19)

Seed scrapings from the inside of 1 vanilla bean

1 extra-large egg, at room temperature

1 extra-large egg yolk, at room temperature

5 ounces (5 squares) unsweetened chocolate, melted and cooled

1 teaspoon pure vanilla extract

Indeed, these cookies are gems: crisp-chewy, buttery, with soft chocolate overtones. The chopped bittersweet chocolate that meanders through the dough forms tiny chocolate "puddles" throughout the baked cookie, giving this sweet a candylike quality.

Cookies made from heaping tablespoons of this dough look homey when piled into a beautiful woven basket and served forth with a pitcher of cold milk. Smaller, teaspoon-size mounds of dough bake into daintier, two-bite–size cookies, and these are lovely piled onto a softly colored pressed glass plate for nibbling with cups of espresso.

———❖❖❖———

Lightly butter and flour 4 cookie sheets, or line the sheets with lengths of cooking parchment paper; set aside. Preheat the oven to 350 degrees.

Resift the cake flour and all-purpose flour with the baking powder, baking soda, salt and cinnamon onto a sheet of wax paper.

Cream the butter in the large bowl of an electric mixer on moderate speed for 2 minutes. Add the granulated sugar in 2 additions, beating for 1 minute after each portion is added. Beat in the vanilla bean scrapings and egg. Beat in the egg yolk and blend well. On low speed, add the melted chocolate, vanilla and chocolate extracts and beat slowly until the chocolate is evenly blended in. On low speed (or by hand), blend in half of the sifted mixture. Blend in all of

1 teaspoon chocolate
   extract
½ cup light cream
1 cup chopped
   bittersweet chocolate

_____

About 50 cookies

the cream, then the remaining sifted mixture. Stir in the chopped bittersweet chocolate.

Drop the dough by rounded tablespoons onto the prepared cookie sheets, placing the mounds 1½ inches apart.

Bake the cookies, one sheet at a time, on the middle-level rack of the oven for 10 to 12 minutes, or until just firm to the touch.

Transfer the cookies to cooling racks, using a wide spatula. Cool for 20 minutes. Store the cookies in an airtight tin.

Applesauce Pillows

2¾ cups *unsifted* all-purpose flour

¾ cup *unsifted* cake flour

1 teaspoon baking soda

¾ teaspoon baking powder

¾ teaspoon salt

2 teaspoons ground cinnamon

1 teaspoon freshly grated nutmeg

½ teaspoon ground ginger

¼ teaspoon ground allspice

¼ teaspoon ground cloves

½ pound (2 sticks) unsalted butter, softened at room temperature

1 cup granulated sugar

¾ cup (firmly packed) light brown sugar

1 extra-large egg, at room temperature

Making cookies with applesauce, spices and molasses has come to be one of my fall baking rituals—along with baking apple breads, apple muffins and apple cakes, and putting up jars of apple butter made with fresh cider.

These cushions of apple goodness are moist, soft and chewy, with raisins. Serve the pillows with a pitcher of hot or cold cider, brewed lemon tea or hot coffee.

———❖❖❖———

Lightly butter and flour 4 cookie sheets, or line the sheets with lengths of cooking parchment paper; set aside. Preheat the oven to 375 degrees.

Sift the all-purpose flour, cake flour, baking soda, baking powder, salt, cinnamon, nutmeg, ginger, allspice and cloves onto a sheet of wax paper.

Cream the butter in the large bowl of an electric mixer on moderate speed for 2 minutes. Add the granulated sugar in 2 additions, beating for 1 minute after each portion is added. Add the light brown sugar and beat for 2 minutes. Beat in the egg and continue beating for 1 minute; add the egg yolk and beat for a minute longer. On low speed, blend in the molasses, applesauce and shredded apple. With the mixer still on low speed (or by hand), blend in the sifted mixture in 2 additions, beating just until the particles of flour have been absorbed. By hand, stir in the raisins and walnuts.

Drop the dough by rounded tablespoons onto the pre-

1 extra-large egg yolk, at
  room temperature

¼ cup light molasses

¾ cup applesauce

½ cup shredded apple
  (about half a medium-
  size apple)

¾ cup dark seedless
  raisins

¾ cup chopped walnuts

About 48 cookies

pared cookie sheets, placing the mounds 2½ inches apart.

Bake the cookies, one sheet at a time, on the middle-level rack of the oven for 11 to 13 minutes, or until just firm to the touch.

Transfer the cookies to cooling racks, using a wide spatula. Cool for 20 minutes. Store the cookies in an airtight tin.

Mint Chocolate Crisps

1½ cups plus
   3 tablespoons *sifted* all-
   purpose flour

¾ teaspoon baking soda

¾ teaspoon salt

12 tablespoons
   (1½ sticks) unsalted
   butter, softened at
   room temperature

1½ cup granulated sugar

1 extra-large egg, at
   room temperature

1 extra-large egg yolk, at
   room temperature

1 teaspoon pure vanilla
   extract

1 teaspoon peppermint
   extract

½ teaspoon chocolate
   extract

2 teaspoons light corn
   syrup

3 ounces (3 squares)
   unsweetened
   chocolate, melted and
   cooled

Enriched with melted unsweetened chocolate, thoroughly loaded with mint-flavored chocolate chips and good butter, this dough makes cookies that are crisp and crunchy. While the cookies are baking, the whole house is filled with an intriguing scent—a combination of mint and chocolate—and before you know it, everyone begins to snatch still-warm cookies from the cooling rack.

Serve the crisps piled into a basket (of woven wood, ceramic or glass) lined with a gingham cloth along with big tumblers of iced coffee or thick vanilla milk shakes.

————— ❖❖❖ —————

Lightly butter and flour 4 cookie sheets, or line the sheets with lengths of cooking parchment paper; set aside. Preheat the oven to 400 degrees.

Resift the flour with the baking soda and salt onto a sheet of wax paper.

Cream the butter in the large bowl of an electric mixer on moderate speed for 2 minutes. Add the granulated sugar in 2 additions, beating for 1 minute after each portion is added. Beat in the egg and egg yolk. Blend in the vanilla, peppermint and chocolate extracts. Slowly blend in the corn syrup and melted chocolate. On low speed (or by hand), add the sifted mixture in 2 additions, beating just until the particles of flour have been absorbed. By hand, fold in the chocolate chips.

Drop the dough by level tablespoons onto the prepared

1½ cups mint-flavored
chocolate chips

_____

About 48 cookies

cookie sheets, placing the mounds 1½ inches apart.

Bake the cookies, one sheet at a time, on the middle-level rack of the oven for 10 to 12 minutes, or until set and just firm to the touch.

Transfer the cookies to cooling racks using a wide spatula. Cool for 20 minutes. Store the cookies in an airtight tin.

Pear–Oatmeal Drops

1½ cups *unsifted* all-purpose flour

¾ cup plus 2 tablespoons *unsifted* cake flour

1¼ teaspoons baking powder

¾ teaspoon baking soda

¾ teaspoon salt

2½ teaspoons ground cinnamon

1 teaspoon freshly grated nutmeg

¾ teaspoon ground ginger

½ teaspoon ground allspice

¼ teaspoon ground cloves

8 tablespoons (1 stick) unsalted butter, softened at room temperature

½ cup shortening

1 cup (firmly packed) light brown sugar

½ cup superfine sugar

These soft mounds are a specialty of my autumn baking kitchen, the season when I love to work with all the harvest fruits and vegetables—pumpkins, cranberries, apples, chestnuts and the entire jewel-like range of dried fruit. Chopped dried pears taste wonderful in this oatmeal cookie, but you can substitute dried peaches or apricots with excellent results.

Pear–Oatmeal Drops look pretty layered in a wooden-ware or wireware basket that has been lined with a checkered or striped tea towel. With the cookies, sip a cup of English Breakfast tea or Hot Spiced Cider (page 133).

————❖❖❖————

Lightly butter and flour 4 cookie sheets, or line the sheets with lengths of cooking parchment paper; set aside. Preheat the oven to 400 degrees.

Sift the all-purpose flour, cake flour, baking powder, baking soda, salt, cinnamon, nutmeg, ginger, allspice and cloves onto a sheet of wax paper.

Cream the butter and shortening in the large bowl of an electric mixer on moderate speed for 2 minutes. Add the light brown sugar and beat for 2 minutes. Add the granulated sugar and beat for 1 minute longer. Beat in the eggs, one at a time, blending well after each addition. Beat in the egg yolks. Blend in the sour cream–vanilla mixture. On low speed (or by hand), add the sifted mixture in 2 additions,

2 extra-large eggs, at
   room temperature
2 extra-large egg yolks,
   at room temperature
¾ cup sour cream
   blended with 2½
   teaspoons pure vanilla
   extract
2¾ cups quick-cooking
   oatmeal
1¾ cups chopped moist
   dried pears
1 cup chopped pecans

About 48 cookies

beating just until the particles of flour have been absorbed. By hand, stir in the oatmeal, pears and pecans.

Drop the dough by rounded tablespoons onto the prepared cookie sheets, placing the mounds 2 inches apart.

Bake the cookies, one sheet at a time, on the middle-level rack of the oven for 12 minutes, or until set, just firm to the touch and light golden.

Transfer the cookies to cooling racks, using a wide spatula. Cool for 20 minutes. Store the cookies in an airtight tin.

Pumpkin–Fig Mounds

2½ cups *unsifted* all-purpose flour

½ cup *unsifted* cake flour

1¼ teaspoons baking powder

¾ teaspoon baking soda

¾ teaspoon salt

2 teaspoons ground cinnamon

1 teaspoon ground ginger

1 teaspoon freshly grated nutmeg

¼ teaspoon ground cloves

¼ teaspoon ground allspice

½ pound (2 sticks) unsalted butter, softened at room temperature

½ cup shortening

1 cup granulated sugar

½ cup (firmly packed) light brown sugar

Several years ago, I baked these cookies a few days before the big Thanksgiving feast. I packed them up, 2 dozen at a time, in shiny tins embossed with autumn leaves. I gave a tin to each guest invited for Thanksgiving dinner—a bread-and-butter gift that was a token of friendship. This was my way of celebrating the harvest. Pumpkin–Fig Mounds taste good accompanied by big cups of mulled wine, Hot Spiced Cider (page 133) or freshly brewed coffee.

———❖❖❖———

Lightly butter and flour 4 cookie sheets, or line the sheets with lengths of cooking parchment paper; set aside. Preheat the oven to 375 degrees.

Sift the all-purpose flour, cake flour, baking powder, baking soda, salt, cinnamon, ginger, nutmeg, cloves and allspice onto a sheet of wax paper.

Cream the butter and shortening in the large bowl of an electric mixer on moderate speed for 2 minutes. Add the granulated sugar and beat for 2 minutes. Add the brown sugar and beat for a minute longer. Beat in the egg and egg yolk. Blend in the vanilla, molasses and pumpkin puree (the mixture may look curdled at this point, and that's okay). On low speed (or by hand), add the sifted mixture in 2 additions, beating just until the particles of flour have been absorbed. By hand, stir in the figs and walnuts.

Drop the dough by rounded tablespoons onto the prepared cookie sheets, placing the mounds 2½ inches apart.

1 extra-large egg, at
room temperature

1 extra-large egg yolk, at
room temperature

2 teaspoons pure vanilla
extract

1 tablespoon light
molasses

1½ cups unsweetened
pumpkin puree

1½ cups stemmed and
chopped dried figs

½ cup chopped walnuts

About 42 cookies

Bake the cookies, one sheet at a time, on the middle-level rack of the oven for 12 to 14 minutes, or until set and just firm to the touch.

Transfer the cookies to cooling racks, using a wide spatula. Cool for 20 minutes. Store the cookies in an airtight tin.

BAKE SALE
GEMS

BAKE SALE GEMS

BAKE SALE BROWNIES

*O*ftentimes, the best of home baking is represented at school bake sales and other charity functions when good cooks contribute cookies, pies and cakes made from scratch. Cookies, it seems, are often snapped up by the dozen, parceled out in clear cellophane bags, sacks or pouches. (And cakes, depending on their size and shape, are sold sliced or whole.)

Those people who love to bake and share their handmade sweets generally use some heirloom recipe that has become a specialty of their kitchen. Over the years, I have baked miniature pound cakes and fruit cakes, plus all sorts of sweet and savory breads. And I have baked dozens and dozens of Grandma Lilly's Brownies (page 64), Chocolate Toffee Squares (page 72), stacks of Lemon Butter Balls (page 58) and huge sheet pans full of Maple Bars (page 52)—all for events that raised funds for increasing benefits and wages for schoolteachers, or for enlarging staffs at day-care centers.

Any of the cookies in this chapter can be made in quantity and held for safekeeping in tightly sealed tins or rigid storage containers. The Double Vanilla "Dog Bones" or Lemon Butter Balls can be tied up in bundles of six or twelve and secured with a curly ribbon. The brownies and bar cookies can be packed individually in plastic wrap, or in neat bundles of four or six and enclosed in heavy cellophane. Individual brownies look appealing stacked in baskets or galvanized steel pails lined with lacy paper doilies.

In addition to the recipes in this chapter, the Ginger Crisps (page 78),

Butterscotch–Granola Discs (page 122), Bittersweet Chocolate–Caramel Bars (page 86), Milk Chocolate–Almond Bars (page 100), Pecan Pie Squares (page 125) or Peanut Delights (page 112) would make a fine contribution to a bake sale. Any of these cookies are a welcome hostess gift: Place the cellophane-wrapped goodies in a good-looking stenciled tin or wooden box lined with fresh lemon or galax leaves.

❖❖❖❖❖❖❖❖❖❖❖❖❖❖❖❖❖

Maple Bars

½ cup *unsifted* all-purpose flour

½ cup *unsifted* cake flour

¼ teaspoon baking powder

¼ teaspoon salt

¼ teaspoon freshly grated nutmeg

8 tablespoons (1 stick) unsalted butter, melted and cooled

¾ cup (firmly packed) light brown sugar

2 extra-large egg yolks, at room temperature

1½ teaspoons pure vanilla extract

Chewy and dense, these bars are a favorite of many people I know who love things like butterscotch brownies, translucent nut pies (especially walnut and pecan) and toffee bars.

Maple Bars can be made in great quantity (this recipe doubles or triples easily) and baked 5 to 6 days before you plan to serve them or sell them at a bake sale. Arrange in bars in shallow tins or heavy plastic containers in 2 layers, separating the top and bottom layer with a sheet of wax paper.

These bars are heavenly with a cup of hot cider, a glass of ice-cold Real Lemonade (page 132) or a mug of freshly brewed coffee.

———❖❖❖———

Lightly butter and flour a 9-inch square baking pan. Line the bottom of the pan with a square of wax paper; set aside. Preheat the oven to 350 degrees.

½ teaspoon maple
   extract
¼ cup pure maple syrup
1 cup chopped walnuts

18 bars

Sift the all-purpose flour, cake flour, baking powder, salt and nutmeg onto a sheet of wax paper.

Whisk the melted butter, brown sugar and egg yolks in a large mixing bowl. Blend in the vanilla and maple extracts. Stir in the maple syrup. Toss the walnuts with 2 teaspoons of the sifted flour mixture in a separate bowl. Stir in the walnuts and the sifted mixture, blending just until the particles of flour have been absorbed.

Spoon the batter into the prepared pan.

Bake on the middle-level rack of the oven for 30 to 35 minutes, or until light golden on top and just firm to the touch. (The entire cake will begin to pull away from the sides of the baking pan when done.)

Cool in the pan on a rack until it reaches room temperature, about 2 hours. Invert onto a second cooling rack, peel away the wax paper and invert again onto a cutting board.

Cut into 18 bars and store them in an airtight tin.

Double Vanilla "Dog Bones"

3½ cups *unsifted* all-purpose flour

½ cup *unsifted* cake flour

2 teaspoons cornstarch

½ teaspoon baking powder

¾ teaspoon salt

1 pound (4 sticks) unsalted butter, softened at room temperature

1 cup plus 2 tablespoons *unsifted* Vanilla-Scented Confectioners' Sugar (page 19)

2½ teaspoons pure vanilla extract

1 tablespoon milk, at room temperature

Seed scrapings from the inside of 1 vanilla bean

One holiday season several years ago, I baked many, many cookies for gifts and to have around the house. Tired of working with cutters in the shape of angels, bells and holly sprigs, I pulled out some whimsical cutters—a pear, a teddy bear, a hand, a foot and a dog bone. I rolled out many batches of the buttery, vanilla-flavored dough given below. I stamped out the sheets of dough with the 3-inch dog bone cutter (it turned out to be the perfect size for these cookies). Friends received their tin of "bones," and every year look forward to these cookies, now a tradition I can't seem to escape.

The "dog bones" are terrific keeping cookies, perfect for making ahead, storing in tins and carrying to bake sales.

Any of the refreshments on pages 132–134 can be offered with a plate of these cookies.

———◆◆◆———

Lightly butter and flour 3 or 4 cookie sheets, or line the sheets with lengths of cooking parchment paper; set aside. Preheat the oven to 350 degrees.

Sift the all-purpose flour, cake flour, cornstarch, baking powder and salt onto a sheet of wax paper.

Cream the butter in the large bowl of an electric mixer on moderate speed for 3 minutes. Add the confectioners' sugar in 2 batches, beating for 1 minute after each portion is added; scrape down the sides of the mixing bowl several times after adding the sugar. Blend in the vanilla extract, milk and vanilla bean scrapings. On low speed (or by hand),

About ⅓ cup Vanilla-
  Scented Granulated
  Sugar (page 19)

About 42 cookies

blend in the sifted mixture in 3 additions, beating just until the particles of flour have been absorbed.

Divide the dough into 2 portions and form each into a rough cake. Roll each cake between sheets of wax paper to a thickness of a scant ½ inch. Refrigerate the sheets of dough on a cookie sheet until they are very firm, about 6 hours. (The sheets of dough can be kept in the refrigerator for up to 3 days before baking; once the dough has firmed up, double-wrap the sheets in plastic wrap.)

Working with one sheet at a time, remove the sheet from the refrigerator and peel off the top layer of wax paper. Stamp out the entire sheet of dough with the dog bone cutter. Remove each cookie from the bottom sheet of wax paper with a small, thin palette knife. Place the cookies 1½ inches apart on the prepared cookie sheets. (Reroll the scraps between sheets of wax paper, chill and cut out more cookies.)

Bake the cookies, one sheet at a time, on the middle-level rack of the oven for 15 minutes, or until pale golden and firm to the touch.

Transfer the cookies to cooling racks using a wide spatula. Sprinkle a little vanilla sugar over the tops of the cookies while they are still warm. Cool for 20 minutes. Store the cookies in an airtight tin.

Chocolate Nut Crunch Squares

FOR THE WALNUT COOKIE LAYER:

1½ cups *unsifted* all-purpose flour

¼ cup *unsifted* cake flour

2 teaspoons cornstarch

¼ teaspoon salt

8 tablespoons (1 stick) unsalted butter, softened at room temperature

½ cup (firmly packed) light brown sugar

¼ teaspoon pure vanilla extract

1 teaspoon milk, at room temperature

¼ cup finely chopped walnuts

These homestyle squares are made up of a crumbly short-breadlike base that's punctuated with chopped walnuts, and a topping of eggs, walnuts, brown sugar and chocolate.

Chocolate Nut Crunch Squares look attractive—and tempting—piled in a shallow basket or in an open cookie tin lined with a pastel-colored tea towel. And remember to take a batch of them on a summer picnic and serve with a windfall of fresh raspberries.

❖❖❖

Lightly butter and flour a 13 x 9 x 2-inch baking pan; set aside. Preheat the oven to 350 degrees.

For the walnut cookie layer, sift the all-purpose flour, cake flour, cornstarch and salt onto a sheet of wax paper.

Cream the butter in the large bowl of an electric mixer on moderate speed for 2 minutes. Add the brown sugar and beat for 1 minute. Add the vanilla and milk and beat for 1 minute longer. On low speed (or by hand), blend in the sifted mixture in 2 additions, beating just until the particles of flour have been absorbed. Stir in the chopped walnuts.

Press the cookie dough evenly on the bottom of the prepared pan. Bake the cookie layer on the middle-level rack of the oven for 15 to 20 minutes, or until an even golden color and firm to the touch. Remove from the oven and set aside on a cooling rack.

For the chocolate and nut topping, combine the brown sugar, granulated sugar, corn syrup, salt, vanilla, egg and egg yolks

FOR THE CHOCOLATE AND
NUT TOPPING:

½ cup (firmly packed)
light brown sugar

¼ cup granulated sugar

¼ cup light corn syrup

¼ teaspoon salt

1 teaspoon pure vanilla
extract

1 extra-large egg, at
room temperature

2 extra-large egg yolks,
at room temperature

1½ cups chopped
walnuts

1 cup chopped
bittersweet chocolate

36 squares

in a large mixing bowl. Beat well. Stir in the chopped walnuts and chocolate.

Spoon the topping evenly over the cookie base. Bake on the middle-level rack of the oven for 20 to 25 minutes, or until the topping is set and firm to the touch.

Cool in the pan on a rack until it reaches room temperature, about 2 hours. Cut into 36 squares and store in an airtight tin.

Lemon Butter Balls

1¾ cups *unsifted* all-purpose flour

¼ cup *unsifted* cake flour

¼ teaspoon baking soda

Pinch of salt

½ pound (2 sticks) unsalted butter, softened at room temperature

½ cup *unsifted* Lemon-Scented Confectioners' Sugar (page 19)

2 teaspoons pure lemon extract

1 tablespoon freshly grated lemon peel

¼ cup ground walnuts

FOR ROLLING THE COOKIES:

About 1½ cups *unsifted* Lemon-Scented Confectioners' Sugar

About 42 cookies

Lemon Butter Balls are softly flavored with finely grated lemon peel, lemon extract and Lemon-Scented Confectioners' Sugar. The dough, which is a joy to work with, can be shaped into crescents and logs in addition to balls. For quantity baking, you can make up several batches of the dough and refrigerate each in a tightly sealed container for up to 5 days. On baking day, remove each package of dough about 15 minutes before you're going to form the balls.

These meltingly rich cookies are just the thing to serve with tall glasses of my Real Lemonade (page 132), Summer Fruit Medley (page 134) or minted iced tea.

———❖❖❖———

Lightly butter and flour 4 cookie sheets, or line the sheets with lengths of cooking parchment paper; set aside. Preheat the oven to 325 degrees.

Sift the all-purpose flour, cake flour, baking soda and salt onto a sheet of wax paper.

Cream the butter in the large bowl of an electric mixer on moderate speed for 2 minutes. Add the confectioners' sugar and beat for 1 minute. Blend in the lemon extract, lemon peel and walnuts. On low speed (or by hand), blend in the sifted mixture in 2 additions, beating just until the particles of flour have been absorbed.

Roll rounded teaspoonfuls of dough into balls. Place the balls 2 inches apart on the prepared cookie sheets.

Bake the cookies, one sheet at a time, on the middle-level rack of the oven for 10 to 12 minutes, or until set and firm to the touch.

Transfer the cookies to cooling racks, using a wide spatula. While the cookies are still warm, roll them in the Lemon-Scented Confectioners' Sugar and return them to the rack. Cool for 20 minutes. Store the cookies in an airtight tin.

Three Nut Bars

FOR THE BROWN SUGAR
COOKIE DOUGH:

1¼ cups *sifted* all-
purpose flour

1 tablespoon cornstarch

¼ teaspoon salt

8 tablespoons (1 stick)
unsalted butter,
softened at room
temperature

½ cup (firmly packed)
light brown sugar

½ teaspoon pure vanilla
extract

½ teaspoon pure almond
extract

In addition to baking panfuls of these rich bars for bake sales, I love to have a few dozen of them stockpiled during the winter holidays. In the late fall, when the fresh crop of nuts abound in the market (in big burlap sacks), buy several pounds of walnuts, pecans and almonds. Freshly cracked nuts keep well in the freezer stored in self-sealing plastic bags and they lend a distinctive taste to this bar cookie.

Rich and satisfying, Three Nut Bars are lovely served with a pot of hot lemon tea, goblets of mulled wine or cold glasses of my Real Lemonade (page 132).

———❖❖❖———

Lightly butter and flour a 10-inch square baking pan; set aside. Preheat the oven to 350 degrees.

For the brown sugar cookie dough, resift the flour with the cornstarch and salt onto a sheet of wax paper.

Cream the butter in the large bowl of an electric mixer on moderate speed for 2 minutes. Add the brown sugar and beat for 1 minute. Blend in the vanilla and almond extracts. On low speed (or by hand), blend in the sifted mixture in 2 additions, beating just until the particles of flour have been absorbed.

Spread the cookie dough evenly on the bottom of the prepared pan. Bake the cookie layer on the middle-level rack for 15 minutes, or until golden and firm to the touch. Remove from the oven and set aside on a cooling rack.

FOR THE NUT TOPPING:

¾ cup (firmly packed) light brown sugar

¼ cup granulated sugar

3 tablespoons *sifted* all-purpose flour

½ teaspoon baking powder

¼ teaspoon salt

1 extra large egg, at room temperature

2 extra-large egg yolks, at room temperature

1 teaspoon pure vanilla extract

1 teaspoon pure almond extract

2 tablespoons unsalted butter, melted and cooled

⅓ cup chopped walnuts

½ cup chopped pecans

½ cup chopped almonds

---

24 bars

For the nut topping, combine the brown sugar, granulated sugar, flour, baking powder and salt in a large mixing bowl. Beat in the egg, egg yolks, vanilla and almond extracts. Blend in the melted butter. Stir in the walnuts, pecans and almonds.

Spoon the topping evenly over the cookie base. Bake on the middle-level rack of the oven for 20 to 25 minutes, or until the topping is set and firm to the touch.

Cool the cake of nut bars on a rack until it reaches room temperature, about 2 hours. Cut into 24 bars and store in an airtight tin.

Coconut Dreams

1 cup *sifted* cake flour

¼ teaspoon baking
powder

½ teaspoon salt

½ teaspoon freshly
grated nutmeg

½ pound (2 sticks)
unsalted butter,
melted and cooled

1 cup (firmly packed)
light brown sugar

⅓ cup granulated sugar

3 extra-large eggs, at
room temperature

2 extra-large egg yolks,
at room temperature

2 teaspoons pure vanilla
extract

2 teaspoons coconut
extract

¼ cup light cream, at
room temperature

2⅔ cups flaked coconut

---

18 squares

Coconut Dreams are chewy and moist—they will remind you of macaroons and blondies. The squares are sweetened by a combination of light brown sugar and granulated sugar, giving them a soft caramel flavor that plays nicely against the coconut. Two good variations of this bar cookie are: macadamia nuts and white chocolate and walnuts and miniature chocolate chips. For the macadamia nut version, decrease the coconut by ⅔ cup and with it fold in 1 cup grated white chocolate and 1 cup chopped macadamia nuts. For the walnut version, decrease the coconut by ⅔ cup and with it fold in 1 cup chopped walnuts and 1 cup miniature semisweet chocolate chips. A tin of Coconut Dreams is a perfect mate to a pitcher of Real Lemonade (page 132).

———❖❖❖———

Lightly butter and flour two 8-inch square baking pans. Line the bottom of each pan with a square of wax paper. Set aside. Preheat the oven to 325 degrees.

Resift the cake flour with the baking powder, salt and nutmeg onto a sheet of wax paper.

Pour the melted butter into a large mixing bowl. Blend in the light brown sugar, granulated sugar, eggs and egg yolks, mixing well. Stir in the vanilla and coconut extracts. Blend in the light cream and coconut.

Spoon the batter into the prepared pans, dividing it evenly between them.

Bake the Dreams on the middle-level rack of the oven for

40 minutes, or until the top of each is golden and just firm to the touch (the cakes will begin to pull away from the sides of the baking pan when done).

Cool each cake in the pan on a rack until it reaches room temperature, about 2 hours. Invert each cake onto a second cooling rack, peel away the wax paper and invert again onto a cutting board.

Cut each cake into 9 squares and store them in an airtight tin.

Moist and fudgy, brownies offered up by the dozen are a favorite bake sale item. They look appealing layered in slatted wooden baskets lined with a cloth or several doilies. All of the recipes that follow have been designed to double successfully if you need an extra big batch. And when I make lots of brownies in advance, I store each cake (the whole block of baked brownie) uncut in a tightly sealed container; several hours or the day before the brownies are needed, I cut each cake into squares or bars.

❖❖❖❖❖❖❖❖❖❖❖❖❖❖❖❖❖❖

Grandma Lilly's Brownies

½ pound (2 sticks) unsalted butter, cut into chunks

4 ounces (4 squares) unsweetened chocolate, chopped

1½ cups *sifted* cake flour

My Grandma Lilly was well known for her brownies (among other tasty things). These chocolate squares are at once cakelike and chewy, and she underbaked them slightly to make them extra fudgy. For years, I'd been terrified of changing the original recipe but knew that reducing the amount of baking powder by half would result in a better brownie, one that was a little more dense. Finally, I altered Grandma's recipe and I think she would approve.

These brownies are usually the first item to sell out at bake sales (they always did when she brought them to such

1 teaspoon baking powder (Grandma used 2 teaspoons)

½ teaspoon salt

½ cup chopped black walnuts

4 extra-large eggs, at room temperature

2 cups Vanilla-Scented Granulated Sugar (page 19)

2 teaspoons pure vanilla extract

---

24 brownies

events when I was in school), so be sure to bake a lot of them.

In my family, it was always traditional to sift confectioners' sugar over the tops of the brownies just before serving.

———— ❖❖❖ ————

Lightly butter and flour a 13 x 9 x 2-inch baking pan; set aside. Preheat the oven to 350 degrees.

Melt the butter and chocolate in a heavy saucepan over very low heat; stir well and set aside to cool.

Resift the cake flour with the baking powder and salt onto a sheet of wax paper. Put the walnuts in a bowl and toss with 1 teaspoon of the sifted mixture.

Pour the melted chocolate–butter mixture into a large mixing bowl. Beat in the eggs, one at a time. Blend in the sugar and vanilla. Stir in the sifted mixture, mixing just until the particles of flour have been absorbed. Fold in the floured walnuts.

Pour and scrape the batter into the prepared pan.

Bake the brownies on the middle-level rack of the oven for 25 minutes (for a *very* fudgy brownie, bake for 20 minutes).

Cool the brownie cake in the pan on a rack until it reaches room temperature, about 2 hours. Cut the cake into 24 squares and store them in an airtight tin.

Heavenly Hash Brownies

12 tablespoons
   (1½ sticks) unsalted
   butter, cut into chunks

4 ounces (4 squares)
   unsweetened
   chocolate, chopped

½ cup *unsifted* all-
   purpose flour

¼ cup *unsifted* cake flour

¼ teaspoon baking
   powder

½ teaspoon salt

½ cup miniature
   semisweet chocolate
   chips

½ cup chopped walnuts

2 extra-large eggs, at
   room temperature

2 extra-large egg yolks,
   at room temperature

1¼ cups Vanilla-Scented
   Granulated Sugar
   (page 19)

2 teaspoons pure vanilla
   extract

These brownies taste like a creamy (and chewy) chocolate and nut candy bar. The buttery batter traps swirls of marsh-mallow cream, miniature chocolate chips and chopped walnuts. For an indulgent dessert, serve the squares warm, topped with a scoop of vanilla ice cream and a spoonful of hot fudge sauce. And to make the ultimate brownie ice cream, cut several brownies into cubes and mash them lightly with the broadside of a knife (or cleaver); fold these chocolate gobs through softened vanilla ice cream and re-freeze for an hour or so. This is delicious.

I serve lots of Heavenly Hash Brownies from an old wide-mouth apothecary jar, with a pot of freshly brewed coffee.

I have baked these brownies for years and years. The brownie batter can hold almost any kind of embellishment you can think of (coconut, macadamia nuts, pecans, chopped caramel or praline) and still bakes up tender and moist inside.

———❖❖❖———

Lightly butter and flour a 9-inch square baking pan. Line the bottom of the pan with a square of wax paper. Set aside. Preheat the oven to 350 degrees.

Melt the butter and chocolate in a heavy saucepan over very low heat; stir well. Set aside to cool.

Sift the all-purpose flour, cake flour, baking powder and salt onto a sheet of wax paper.

1 teaspoon chocolate
extract

½ cup marshmallow
cream

_____

9 large brownies

Combine the chocolate chips and walnuts in a small bowl and toss with 2 teaspoons of the sifted flour mixture.

Beat the eggs and egg yolks in a large mixing bowl. Whisk in the granulated sugar, vanilla and chocolate extracts. Blend in the cooled butter–chocolate mixture. Stir in the sifted mixture, blending just until the particles of flour have been absorbed. Fold in the chocolate chips and walnuts. Spoon the marshmallow cream on top of the chocolate batter and swirl it in with a few quick strokes (leave the cream in rather large patches to prevent it from dissolving into the batter).

Carefully pour and scrape the batter into the prepared pan.

Bake the brownies on the middle-level rack of the oven for 40 to 45 minutes, or until the brownie cake begins to pull away from the sides of the baking pan.

Cool the cake in the pan on a rack until it reaches room temperature, about 2 hours. Invert the cake onto a second cooling rack, peel away the wax paper and invert again onto a cutting board.

Cut the brownie cake into 9 squares and store them in an airtight tin.

Double Chocolate–Walnut Fudgies

½ pound (2 sticks) unsalted butter, cut into chunks

6 ounces (6 squares) unsweetened chocolate, chopped

½ cup *unsifted* cake flour

½ cup *unsifted* all-purpose flour

1 teaspoon salt

1 cup chopped walnuts

⅔ cup miniature semisweet chocolate chips

3 extra-large eggs, at room temperature

2 extra-large egg yolks, at room temperature

2 cups Vanilla-Scented Granulated Sugar (page 19)

2½ teaspoons pure vanilla extract

1 teaspoon chocolate extract

Fudgies are moist, candylike squares packed with a double dose of chocolate—melted unsweetened chocolate colors the batter while semisweet chocolate chips add little pockets of chocolate richness. These are easy to pack and carry in the lunch bag or box if wrapped securely in wax paper or popped into self-sealing plastic pouches. At home, sprinkle the walnut-flecked tops of the fudgies with a light sifting of confectioners' sugar and serve with a pot of steaming hot coffee or pitcher of milk.

————❖❖❖————

Lightly butter and flour two 8-inch square baking pans. Line the bottom of each pan with a square of wax paper; set aside. Preheat the oven to 350 degrees.

Melt the butter and chocolate in a heavy saucepan over very low heat; stir well. Set aside to cool.

Sift the cake flour, all-purpose flour and salt onto a sheet of wax paper.

Combine the walnuts and chocolate chips in a small bowl and toss with 1 tablespoon of the sifted flour mixture.

Beat the eggs and egg yolks in a large mixing bowl. Blend in the granulated sugar and mix well. Blend in the vanilla and chocolate extracts. Stir in the melted chocolate–butter mixture. Stir in the sifted mixture, blending just until the particles of flour have been absorbed. Fold in the chocolate chips and walnuts.

Spoon the batter into the prepared pans, dividing it

⅔ cup chopped walnuts

---

18 brownies

evenly between them. Sprinkle the top of each pan of batter with ⅓ cup chopped walnuts.

Bake the Fudgies on the middle-level rack of the oven for 40 minutes, until the top is set and shiny, and each cake pulls away slightly from the sides of the baking pan.

Cool each cake in the pan on a rack until it reaches room temperature, about 2 hours. Invert each cake onto a second cooling rack, peel away the wax paper and invert again onto a cutting board.

Cut each cake into 9 squares and store them in an airtight tin.

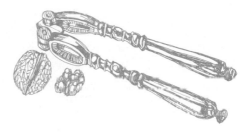

Coconut–
Chocolate
"Swirlies"

½ pound (2 sticks)
unsalted butter,
softened at room
temperature

4 ounces (4 squares)
unsweetened
chocolate, chopped

1¼ cups *sifted* cake flour

1 tablespoon *unsifted*
unsweetened cocoa
powder

½ teaspoon salt

3 extra-large eggs, at
room temperature

2 extra-large egg yolks,
at room temperature

2 cups Vanilla-Scented
Granulated Sugar
(page 19)

2 teaspoons pure vanilla
extract

1 teaspoon chocolate
extract

"Swirlies" are like brownies, but better: drifts of marshmallow cream and flaked coconut wind through the chocolate batter in an intriguing pattern. I have been baking this brownie-like confection for many, many years; I've taken them to country fairs and bazaars, teas, picnics and charity events. They are a toothsome lunch box or picnic dessert.

Serve a big plate of "Swirlies" with tall glasses of strong iced coffee, a pot of hot coffee or pitcher of cold milk.

Lightly butter and flour two 8-inch square baking pans. Line the bottom of each pan with a square of wax paper; set aside. Preheat the oven to 350 degrees.

Melt the butter and chocolate in a heavy saucepan over very low heat; stir well. Set aside to cool.

Resift the cake flour with the cocoa and salt onto a sheet of wax paper. Beat the eggs and egg yolks in a large mixing bowl. Blend in the granulated sugar and mix well. Beat in the vanilla and chocolate extracts. Blend in the cooled chocolate–butter mixture. Stir in the sifted mixture, blending just until the particles of flour have been absorbed. Spoon the marshmallow cream on top of the chocolate batter, sprinkle over the flaked coconut and swirl both in with a few quick strokes of a wooden spoon (leave the cream in patches to prevent it from dissolving into the batter).

Pour and scrape the batter into the prepared pans, dividing it evenly between them.

¾ cup marshmallow
 cream
½ cup flaked coconut

---

18 brownies

Bake the "Swirlies" on the middle-level rack of the oven for 35 to 40 minutes, until the top is set and each cake pulls away slightly from the sides of the baking pan.

Cool each cake of "Swirlies" in the pan on a rack until it reaches room temperature, about 2 hours. Invert each cake onto a second cooling rack, peel away the wax paper and invert again onto a cutting board.

Cut each cake into 9 squares and store them in an airtight tin.

Chocolate Toffee Squares

1¼ cups *unsifted* all-purpose flour

¼ cup *unsifted* cake flour

¾ teaspoon baking powder

½ teaspoon salt

1 cup *unsifted* unsweetened cocoa powder

¾ pound (3 sticks) unsalted butter, melted and cooled

1 square (1 ounce) unsweetened chocolate, melted

5 extra-large eggs, at room temperature

1 extra-large egg yolk, at room temperature

2 tablespoons milk, at room temperature

2 tablespoons light corn syrup

2 teaspoons pure vanilla extract

1 teaspoon chocolate extract

These thick squares are rich in chocolate; chopped chocolate-covered toffee bars get stirred through a buttery cocoa batter, and more chopped toffee is sprinkled on top right before baking. My mother baked these brownies frequently; this is my version of her recipe. (I've added chocolate extract for a full chocolate bouquet and use Vanilla-Scented Granulated Sugar.) The squares are quite moist and tender; they keep very well at room temperature when packed in a tightly sealed tin. If you are making the squares to sell at a bake sale, wrap each in clear cellophane and arrange them in shallow baskets. At home, I present these fudgy wonders in an antique cake tin or cookie box lined with heart-shaped doilies.

Chocolate Toffee Squares are delicious served with cups of hot coffee, tall glasses of iced coffee or cold milk.

Lightly butter and flour a 13 x 9 x 2-inch baking pan. Line the bottom with a square of wax paper. Set aside. Preheat the oven to 350 degrees.

Sift the all-purpose flour, cake flour, baking powder, salt and cocoa onto a sheet of wax paper.

Whisk the melted butter, chocolate, eggs, egg yolk and milk in a large mixing bowl. Blend in the corn syrup, vanilla and chocolate extracts. Beat in the granulated sugar.

Put the chopped toffee candy in a bowl and toss with 2 teaspoons of the sifted dry ingredients. Stir the sifted mixture into the egg and sugar mixture, mixing just until the

2⅔ cups Vanilla-Scented
   Granulated Sugar
   (page 19)
6 packages (1.20 ounces
   each) chocolate-
   covered toffee bars
   (such as Heath Bars),
   chopped (about
   1¼ cups)

FOR SPRINKLING:

4 packages (1.20 ounces
   each) chocolate-
   covered toffee bars,
   chopped (about
   ¾ cup)

About 32 brownies

particles of flour have been absorbed. Fold in the floured chopped toffee.

Spoon the batter into the prepared pan. Sprinkle the chopped toffee candy on top of the batter.

Bake the squares on the middle-level rack of the oven for 40 minutes, or until the cake begins to pull away from the sides of the baking pan.

Cool the cake in the pan on a rack until it reaches room temperature, about 2 hours. Invert the cake onto a second cooling rack, peel away the wax paper and invert again onto a cutting board.

Cut the cake into 32 squares and store them in an airtight tin.

Baking Note: My mother also made marvelous brownies using almond butter crunch, chopped up and folded through the dense batter. To vary this recipe, you can substitute the same amount of almond butter crunch candy for the toffee; then substitute 1 teaspoon pure almond extract for the chocolate extract called for in the recipe.

LUNCH BOX
COOKIES

LUNCH BOX COOKIES

———— ❖·❖·❖ ————

*C*ookies that get packed up in lunch boxes should satisfy that craving for something sweet, whether they are crisp and buttery (like my Sugar Cookie Hearts on page 84), or substantial and hearty (like my Pecan Butter Crunch Squares on page 82 or the Oatmeal–Raisin Saucers on page 88).

The cookies in this chapter are good for munching on during the afternoon, with or without a piece of fresh fruit. The Bittersweet Chocolate–Caramel Bars rely on the combination of butter and chocolate to keep them moist and tasty, so they can be made over the weekend and enjoyed for days to follow (if they last that long). The Ginger Crisps, Apple Butter Cookies and Pumpkin–Spice Cookies contain lots of spices and the usual "goods on hand" that cookie bakers keep stocked in the pantry.

These cookies are perfect for stashing in the lunch box or briefcase because they are a full-flavored, easy-to-carry sweet—and much more delicious than a packaged candy bar! Any of the fruit and spice cookies would be a nourishing dessert for school-bound children; the cookies taste good after a sandwich or thermos of soup.

Also, remember that the Pecan Butter Crunch Squares are a welcome addition to boxed picnic lunches, along with some fresh seasonal fruit such as plums, peaches and nectarines. Wrap the squares in clear cellophane wrap before packing them.

Besides the cookies in this chapter, there are many others in this book that are handy to have ready-made and in the cupboard for tucking into lunch boxes. Among them: Mint Chocolate Crisps (page 42), Heavenly Hash Brownies (page 66), Chocolate Toffee Squares (page 72), Maple Bars (page 52), Chocolate Nut Crunch Squares (page 56), Peanut Delights (page 112), Butterscotch–Granola Discs (page 122), Fruit Clusters (page 120), Banana–Oatmeal Pillows (page 114), Sour Cream–Molasses–Spice Rounds (page 118) and Grandma Lilly's Brownies (page 64).

❖❖❖❖❖❖❖❖❖❖❖❖❖❖❖❖❖❖

Ginger Crisps

2¾ cups *sifted* all-purpose flour

¼ cup plus 1 tablespoon *sifted* cake flour

1 tablespoon baking soda

¾ teaspoon salt

2½ teaspoons ground ginger

2 teaspoons ground cinnamon

½ teaspoon ground allspice

¼ teaspoon ground cloves

¼ teaspoon freshly grated nutmeg

One of my favorite ginger cookies, these wafers really snap when you bite into them. Ground ginger is the keynote of the spices, of course, but its flavor is supported by aromatic ground cinnamon, allspice, cloves and nutmeg.

Keep Ginger Crisps in the cookie jar for friends and family to snack on. And when a dessert of baked or poached fruit—particularly apples and pear—calls for something crisp and spicy as an accompaniment, remember these cookies.

Ginger Crisps are delicious paired with glasses of Real Lemonade (page 132), mulled wine or Hot Spiced Cider (page 133).

———❖❖❖———

Lightly butter and flour 4 cookie sheets, or line the sheets with lengths of cooking parchment paper; set aside. Preheat the oven to 375 degrees.

1 cup plus 2 tablespoons
shortening

1⅓ cups superfine sugar

2 tablespoons (firmly
packed) light brown
sugar

5 tablespoons light
molasses

1 extra-large egg, at
room temperature

1 extra-large egg yolk, at
room temperature

1 teaspoon milk

1½ teaspoons pure
vanilla extract

FOR ROLLING THE COOKIES:

1 cup granulated sugar
blended with
1 teaspoon ground
ginger

About 50 cookies

Resift the all-purpose and cake flours with the baking soda, salt, ginger, cinnamon, allspice, cloves and nutmeg onto a sheet of wax paper.

Cream the shortening in the large bowl of an electric mixer on moderate speed for 2 minutes. Add the superfine sugar in 2 additions, beating for 1 minute after each portion is added. Beat in the light brown sugar. Add the molasses and beat for 1 minute. Add the egg and egg yolk; beat for 1 minute. Blend in the milk and vanilla extract. On low speed (or by hand), add the sifted mixture in 2 additions, beating just until the particles of flour have been absorbed.

Roll level tablespoons of dough into balls. Roll each ball in the ginger-spiced sugar. Place the balls 2½ inches apart on the prepared cookie sheets. (The dough is soft, so in very hot or humid weather, refrigerate it for 1 hour, or until just firm enough to roll.)

Bake the cookies, one sheet at a time, on the middle-level rack of the oven for 12 to 14 minutes, or until set and firm to the touch (the dough will rise up during baking, then flatten and firm up).

Transfer the cookies to cooling racks, using a wide spatula. Cool for 20 minutes. Store the cookies in an airtight tin.

Apple Butter Cookies

3 cups *sifted* all-purpose flour

1 cup plus 2 tablespoons *sifted* cake flour

1 teaspoon baking soda

1 teaspoon baking powder

1 teaspoon salt

2½ teaspoons ground cinnamon

1¼ teaspoons freshly grated nutmeg

¾ teaspoon ground ginger

½ teaspoon ground allspice

¼ teaspoon ground cloves

12 tablespoons (1½ sticks) unsalted butter, softened at room temperature

¼ cup shortening

1 cup (firmly packed) light brown sugar

⅓ cup superfine sugar

Every fall, I put up jars of silky apple butter to use as a spread for muffins, toast and sweet yeast breads, and to add to holiday fruit cakes and pie fillings. Apple butter (as well as peach, pear or cranberry butter) lends an incomparable satiny quality to many baked goods. Cookies made with apple butter bake up golden, with a fine crumb and delectable flavor.

These Apple Butter Cookies are spicy and soft, and they are a fine accompaniment for a helping of poached fruit. A heap of cookies, presented in an old wicker basket, is just the right thing to serve with cups of hot buttered rum or freshly brewed coffee.

———❖❖❖———

Lightly butter and flour 4 cookie sheets, or line the sheets with lengths of cooking parchment paper; set aside. Preheat the oven to 375 degrees.

Resift the all-purpose and cake flour with the baking soda, baking powder, salt, cinnamon, nutmeg, ginger, allspice and cloves onto a sheet of wax paper.

Cream the butter and shortening in the large bowl of an electric mixer on moderate speed for 2 minutes. Add the light brown sugar and beat for 1 minute. Add the superfine sugar and beat for a minute longer. Add the egg and beat for 1 minute; add the egg yolks and beat for a minute longer. Blend in the apple butter, sour cream and shredded apple. On low speed (or by hand) blend in the sifted mix-

1 extra-large egg, at
   room temperature

2 extra-large egg yolks,
   at room temperature

½ cup apple butter

2 tablespoons sour
   cream

1½ cups (firmly packed)
   shredded tart cooking
   apples (about
   2 medium size)

½ cup chopped pecans

½ cup dried currants

About 48 cookies

ture in 3 additions, beating just until the particles of flour have been absorbed. By hand, stir in the pecans and currants.

Drop the dough by rounded tablespoons onto the prepared cookie sheets, placing the mounds 2½ inches apart.

Bake the cookies, a sheet at a time, on the middle-level rack of the oven for 12 to 13 minutes, or until firm to the touch.

Transfer the cookies to cooling racks, using a wide spatula. Cool for 20 minutes. Store the cookies in an airtight tin.

Baking Note: This recipe has been in my file for many cookie-baking years. My grandmother made them with applesauce (instead of the apple butter) and golden raisins (instead of the currants). I add a little sour cream to smooth out the cookie dough and sift lots of spices with the flour.

Pecan Butter Crunch Squares

1 ¼ cups *unsifted* all-purpose flour

¼ cup *unsifted* cake flour

½ teaspoon baking soda

½ teaspoon baking powder

½ teaspoon salt

¾ teaspoon freshly grated nutmeg

¼ teaspoon ground allspice

8 tablespoons (1 stick) unsalted butter, melted and cooled

2 tablespoons shortening, melted and cooled

1 ½ cups (firmly packed) brown sugar

½ cup granulated sugar

1 extra-large egg, at room temperature

2 extra-large egg yolks, at room temperature

1 teaspoon pure vanilla extract

Soft and chewy, these pecan butter squares are easily mixed in a large bowl. The topping is a sweet and crunchy finish to the cookies: the crumble of brown sugar, butter and chopped pecans caramelizes lightly during baking, adding another texture.

In the summertime, arrange Pecan Butter Crunch Squares in a willow basket and serve with fresh seasonal berries (such as a mixture of blackberries, raspberries and blueberries); in fall and winter, accompany the squares with a bowl of homemade applesauce or poached pears.

Lightly butter and flour a 9-inch square baking pan. Line the bottom of the pan with a square of wax paper; set aside. Preheat the oven to 350 degrees.

Sift the all-purpose flour, cake flour, baking soda, baking powder, salt, nutmeg and allspice onto a large sheet of wax paper.

Combine the butter and shortening in a large mixing bowl. Stir in the brown sugar and granulated sugar. Beat in the egg and egg yolks. Blend in the vanilla and maple extracts. Add the sifted mixture, sprinkle over the pecans and blend everything together until the particles of flour have been absorbed.

Spoon the batter into the prepared pan, spreading it into the corners and smoothing over the top.

For the pecan–sugar topping, combine the pecans, light

½ teaspoon maple
extract

1½ cups chopped pecans

FOR THE PECAN—SUGAR
TOPPING:

½ cup chopped pecans

1 tablespoon (firmly
packed) light brown
sugar

1 tablespoon unsalted
butter, melted and
cooled

12 squares

brown sugar and butter in a small mixing bowl. Crumble
everything together with your fingertips and sprinkle
evenly over the pan of batter.

Bake the crunches on the middle-level rack of the oven
for 25 minutes, or until the top is set and the cake pulls
away slightly from the sides of the baking pan.

Cool the cake in the pan on a rack until it reaches room
temperature, about 2 hours. Carefully invert the cake onto
a second cooling rack, peel away the wax paper and invert
again onto a cutting board.

Cut the cake into 12 squares and store them in an airtight tin.

Sugar Cookie Hearts

4½ cups *unsifted* all-purpose flour

¾ teaspoon baking powder

⅛ teaspoon baking soda

1 teaspoon salt

½ teaspoon freshly grated nutmeg

¾ pound (3 sticks) unsalted butter, softened at room temperature

2¼ cups Vanilla-Scented Granulated Sugar (page 19)

2 extra-large eggs, at room temperature

2 extra-large egg yolks, at room temperature

2½ teaspoons pure vanilla extract

Seed scrapings from the inside of ½ a vanilla bean

2 tablespoons plus 1 teaspoon milk, at room temperature

I am partial to baking cookies, muffins, rolls and miniature pastries in the shape of hearts. I always cut out sheets of this thin cookie dough with an antique heart-shaped cutter: it has finely scalloped edges and makes beautiful cookies.

Sugar Cookie Hearts are wonderful to have on hand for adding to lunch bags, and the holiday cookie basket would not be complete without them.

In the summer, serve the cookies with Real Lemonade (page 132).

———❖❖❖———

Sift the all-purpose flour, baking powder, baking soda, salt and nutmeg onto a sheet of wax paper.

Cream the butter in the large bowl of an electric mixer on moderate speed for 3 minutes. Add the sugar in 3 additions, beating for 1 minute after each portion is added; scrape down the sides of the mixing bowl frequently. Beat in the eggs, one at a time, blending well after each addition. Beat in the egg yolks. Blend in the vanilla extract, vanilla bean scrapings and milk. On low speed (or by hand), blend in the sifted mixture in 3 additions, beating just until the particles of flour have been absorbed.

Divide the dough into 3 portions and form each into a rough cake. Roll each cake between sheets of wax paper to a thickness of ¼ inch. Freeze the sheets of dough stacked on cookie sheets until they are very firm, about 3 to 4 hours. (The sheets of dough can be kept in the freezer for up to 1 week before cutting and baking; once the dough has firmed

About ⅔ cup Vanilla-
  Scented Granulated
  Sugar (page 19)

About 72 cookies

up, double-wrap the sheets in plastic wrap and aluminum foil.)

Lightly butter and flour 4 cookie sheets, or line the sheets with lengths of cooking parchment paper; set aside. Preheat the oven to 375 degrees.

Stamp out each sheet of dough with a 3-inch heart-shaped cutter. Place the cookies 1–1½ inches apart on the prepared cookie sheets. (Reroll the scraps between sheets of wax paper, chill and cut out more cookies.) Sprinkle the cookies lightly with the Vanilla-Scented Granulated Sugar.

Bake the cookies, one sheet at a time, on the middle-level rack of the oven for 10 to 12 minutes, or until light golden and firm to the touch.

Transfer the cookies to cooling racks, using a wide spatula. Cool for 20 minutes. Store the cookies in an airtight tin.

Baking Note: Prior to freezing, this cookie dough is quite sticky. Once the sheets of dough are frozen firm, the dough is easy to stamp out with a cutter and holds its shape nicely during baking. Although you might be tempted, adding additional flour to the dough will spoil the texture and make the cookies a lot less delicate-crisp than they should be. Freezing the dough takes care of the handling, and the baked cookies will be light and tender as a result.

Bittersweet Chocolate– Caramel Bars

1¾ cups *unsifted* all-purpose flour

¼ cup *unsifted* cake flour

¼ teaspoon salt

½ pound (2 sticks) unsalted butter, softened at room temperature

¾ cup (firmly packed) light brown sugar

¼ cup granulated sugar

2 extra-large egg yolks, at room temperature

1 teaspoon pure vanilla extract

1 cup vanilla caramels

4 tablespoons milk

1¼ cups chopped bittersweet chocolate

¾ cup chopped walnuts, lightly toasted

---

48 bars

All the good larder ingredients—chocolate, butter, brown sugar, eggs and walnuts—are combined to make a bar cookie that's sweet and crunchy-chewy. A butter cookie dough made with brown sugar and egg yolks forms the base for a topping of chopped bittersweet chocolate, walnuts and caramel. These are rich.

Offer a plate of Bittersweet Chocolate–Caramel Bars with bowls of plain vanilla ice cream, mousse or a summer compote of fresh berries.

————❖❖❖————

Lightly butter and flour a 15 x 10 x 1-inch jelly roll pan; set aside. Preheat the oven to 350 degrees.

Blend together the all-purpose flour, cake flour and salt in a mixing bowl.

Cream the butter in the large bowl of an electric mixer on moderate speed for 2 minutes. Add the light brown sugar and beat for 1 minute. Add the granulated sugar and beat for a minute longer. Beat in the egg yolks. Blend in the vanilla. On low speed (or by hand), blend in the flour mixture in 2 additions, mixing just until the particles of flour have been absorbed.

Press the cookie dough evenly on the bottom of the prepared pan. Bake the cookie layer on the middle-level rack of the oven for 15 to 20 minutes, or until golden and firm to the touch. Leave the oven on.

In the meantime, melt the caramels with the milk in a saucepan, stirring occasionally; keep warm.

As soon as the cookie dough has been removed from the oven, scatter the chopped chocolate evenly over the top. Return to the oven for 1 to 2 minutes longer, or until the chocolate has softened. Gently spread the chocolate in large patches over the top of the cookie dough, leaving small spaces of the dough showing. Drizzle the melted caramel over with a teaspoon, then sprinkle with chopped walnuts.

Cool the cake in the pan on a rack until it reaches room temperature, about 2 hours. Cut into 48 bars with a sharp knife and store them in an airtight tin.

Baking Note: In very hot or humid weather, or if your kitchen is warm, it may be necessary to chill the pan of bars before cutting to firm up the chocolate and caramel. Place the pan in the refrigerator for 1 hour or in the freezer for about 15 to 20 minutes.

Oatmeal–Raisin Saucers

2½ cups *unsifted* all-purpose flour

½ cup *unsifted* cake flour

2 teaspoons baking soda

1 teaspoon baking powder

1 teaspoon salt

1½ teaspoons ground cinnamon

1 teaspoon freshly grated nutmeg

1 cup shortening, melted and cooled

8 tablespoons (1 stick) unsalted butter, melted and cooled

2 cups (firmly packed) light brown sugar

1 cup granulated sugar

2 extra-large eggs, at room temperature

2 extra-large egg yolks, at room temperature

2 teaspoons pure vanilla extract

These saucers are thin and chewy, with a soft butterscotch flavor. The ground cinnamon and nutmeg gently spice the oatmeal-coconut-raisin dough. Still warm from the oven and fragrant, the cookies are easy to devour along with a glass of cold milk or a cup of tea.

Lightly butter and flour 4 cookie sheets, or line the sheets with lengths of cooking parchment paper; set aside. Preheat the oven to 350 degrees.

Sift the all-purpose flour, cake flour, baking soda, baking powder, salt, cinnamon and nutmeg onto a sheet of wax paper.

Whisk the shortening and butter together in a large mixing bowl. Stir in the brown sugar and granulated sugar. Beat in the eggs, one at a time; beat in the egg yolks. Blend in the vanilla. Blend in the sifted mixture in 2 additions, stirring just until the particles of flour have been absorbed. Stir in the oatmeal, coconut and raisins.

Drop the dough by heaping tablespoons onto the prepared cookie sheets, placing the mounds 3 inches apart.

Bake the cookies, a sheet at a time, on the middle-level rack of the oven for 12 to 15 minutes, or until just set (the cookies will be slightly soft on top).

2½ cups quick-cooking
oatmeal

1¾ cups flaked coconut

1 cup dark seedless
raisins

About 60 cookies

Transfer the cookies to cooling racks, using a wide spatula. Cool for 20 minutes. Store the cookies in an airtight tin.

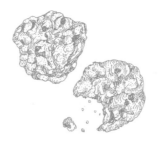

❖·❖·❖·❖·❖·❖·❖·❖·❖·❖·❖·❖·❖·❖

Pumpkin–Spice Cookies

2 cups *unsifted* all-
purpose flour

½ cup *unsifted* cake flour

1 teaspoon baking soda

1 teaspoon baking
powder

¾ teaspoon salt

2 teaspoons ground
cinnamon

¾ teaspoon freshly
grated nutmeg

Pumpkin puree and a mingling of five pungent spices create a few dozen moist and ruddy-colored cookies. These are soft mounds, packed with chewy dates and chopped cashews. For body and substance, I like to add a few spoonfuls of bran to the dough. Pumpkin–Spice Cookies go well with Hot Spiced Cider (page 133), rum toddies or cold milk.

❖·❖·❖ ————

Lightly butter and flour 3 cookie sheets, or line the sheets with lengths of cooking parchment paper; set aside. Preheat the oven to 375 degrees.

Sift the all-purpose flour, cake flour, baking soda, baking

½ teaspoon ground
ginger

¼ teaspoon ground
allspice

¼ teaspoon ground
cloves

8 tablespoons (1 stick)
unsalted butter,
softened at room
temperature

8 tablespoons shortening

1 cup (firmly packed)
light brown sugar

1 extra-large egg, at
room temperature

1 extra-large egg yolk, at
room temperature

1 tablespoon molasses

2 teaspoons pure vanilla
extract

1 cup unsweetened
pumpkin puree

¾ cup chopped pitted
dates

¾ cup chopped unsalted
cashews

3 tablespoons bran

About 36 cookies

powder, salt, cinnamon, nutmeg, ginger, allspice and cloves
onto a sheet of wax paper.

Cream the butter and shortening in the large bowl of an
electric mixer on moderate speed for 2 minutes. Add the
sugar and beat for 1 minute. Beat in the egg and egg yolk.
Blend in the molasses and vanilla. Add the pumpkin puree
and blend well. On low speed (or by hand), blend in the
sifted mixture in 2 additions, beating just until the particles
of flour have been absorbed. By hand, stir in the dates,
cashews and bran.

Drop the dough by rounded tablespoons onto the prepared cookie sheets, placing the mounds 2½ inches apart.

Bake the cookies, one sheet at a time, on the middle-level
rack of the oven for 12 to 14 minutes, or until firm to the
touch.

Transfer the cookies to cooling racks, using a wide spatula. Cool 20 minutes. Store the cookies in an airtight tin.

COFFEE AND TEA
SWEETS

Wendy Wheeler

COFFEE AND TEA SWEETS

———————— ❖❖❖ ————————

I love to set out a coffee or tea service with sweets on a well-worn pine table in my library. (The library is a cozy place—where a jumble of books and lots of porcelain collected over the years fills all the nooks.) I decorate the table with all the expected accompaniments, and a few unexpected things, too: a pitcher of cream and bowl of sugar, a plate of lemon slices (if tea is served), embroidered napkins, pastel china plates, a dish of homemade potpourri to scent the room or a posy of dried flowers.

For the coffee or tea hour, it's a nice gesture to offer at least two different kinds of cookies and present them in an appealing way. Arrange them in baskets, in napkin-lined tins or in fancy copper molds. Make a simple fresh fruit compote, if you like, and serve that with a bowl of softly whipped cream for spooning over.

The cookies in this chapter are crisp and buttery, soft and chewy or firm and not too sweet—in my house, they are the traditional accompaniments to coffee or tea. The Giant Double Chocolate Rounds are 9-inch circles of dough laced with miniature chocolate chips and baked in shallow tart pans. This is a break-apart cookie, meant for guests to nibble on a little at a time. The Cinnamon–Cashew "Dunking" Cookies and the Chocolate Chip Rusks are crisp and softly flavored—ideal for dipping into cups of steamy hot cappuccino or strong coffee.

Many cookies that are ideal for filling the cookie jar or bringing to a bake sale (from the Cookie Jar Treats and Bake Sale Gems chapters) are equally good to serve with coffee or tea. They are: the Vanilla Melt-a-Ways (page 32), Chocolate Gems (page 38), Mint Chocolate Crisps (page 42), Chocolate Toffee Squares (page 72), Maple Bars (page 52), Double Vanilla "Dog Bones" (page 54), Lemon Butter Balls (page 58), Three Nut Bars (page 60) and Coconut Dreams (page 62).

❖❖❖❖❖❖❖❖❖❖❖❖❖❖❖❖❖

Black Walnut Butter Drops

1¾ cups *unsifted* all-purpose flour

¼ cup *unsifted* cake flour

¼ teaspoon baking powder

½ teaspoon salt

½ teaspoon freshly grated nutmeg

½ pound (2 sticks) unsalted butter, softened at room temperature

1 cup Vanilla-Scented Granulated Sugar (page 19)

Simple and sweet, these butter drops have a cakelike texture —which makes them delicate little mouthfuls. Bits of black walnuts wind through each cookie, for flavor and crunch. Apart from serving with hot coffee or iced tea to regenerate the spirit in the morning or afternoon, the cookies are a welcome accompaniment to mousse, ice cream or fruit salad.

———❖❖❖———

Lightly butter and flour 4 cookie sheets, or line the sheets with lengths of cooking parchment paper; set aside. Preheat the oven to 300 degrees.

Sift the all-purpose flour, cake flour, baking powder, salt and nutmeg onto a sheet of wax paper.

Cream the butter in the large bowl of an electric mixer on moderate speed for 2 minutes. Add the sugar in 2 additions,

2 teaspoons pure vanilla
  extract
1 extra-large egg, at
  room temperature
¾ cup chopped black
  walnuts (English
  walnuts may be
  substituted)

About 48 cookies

beating for 1 minute after each portion is added. Beat in the vanilla and egg. On low speed (or by hand), add the sifted mixture in 2 additions, beating just until the particles of flour have been absorbed. By hand, stir in the walnuts.

Drop the dough by rounded teaspoons onto the prepared cookie sheets, placing the mounds 1 inch apart.

Bake the cookies, one sheet at a time, on the middle-level rack of the oven for 20 to 25 minutes, or until very pale golden and firm to the touch.

Transfer the cookies to cooling racks, using a wide spatula. Store the cookies in an airtight tin.

Baking Note: This recipe was my mother's. She added golden raisins (¼ cup) to the dough along with the walnuts, and used 2 cups of all-purpose flour.

Giant Double Chocolate Rounds

2¾ cups *unsifted* all-purpose flour

¼ cup *unsifted* cake flour

1 teaspoon cornstarch

¾ cup *unsifted* unsweetened cocoa powder

¼ teaspoon baking soda

⅛ teaspoon baking powder

½ teaspoon salt

¾ pound (3 sticks) unsalted butter, softened at room temperature

1½ cups Vanilla-Scented Confectioners' Sugar (page 19)

2 teaspoons pure vanilla extract

½ teaspoon chocolate extract

2 teaspoons light cream, at room temperature

This recipe makes two huge buttery chocolate cookies, flecked with miniature chocolate chips. The dough is pressed into fluted metal tart pans with removable bottoms and baked; what you pull from the oven are firm, yet meltingly rich discs, perfect for nibbling on with coffee or tea.

The rounds look pretty sitting on a flat, doily-lined plate, with sprigs of fresh lavender, holly or apple blossom encircling the cookie. Giant Double Chocolate Rounds are wonderful to take on a picnic or to offer at an *al fresco* supper, accompanied by a bowl of fresh cherries.

With nonstick cookware spray, spray the inside of two 9-inch tart pans with removable bottoms. Line the bottom of the pans with a circle of wax paper or parchment paper; set aside. Preheat the oven to 325 degrees.

Sift the all-purpose flour, cake flour, cornstarch, cocoa, baking soda, baking powder and salt onto a sheet of wax paper.

Cream the butter in the large bowl of an electric mixer on moderate speed for 2 minutes. Add the Vanilla-Scented Confectioners' Sugar and beat for 2 minutes, scraping down the sides of the mixing bowl frequently. Blend in the vanilla and chocolate extracts and light cream. On low speed (or by hand), blend in the sifted mixture in 3 additions, beating just until the particles of flour have been absorbed. By hand, stir in the chocolate chips.

¾ cup miniature
  semisweet chocolate
  chips

FOR SPRINKLING:

About 1½ tablespoons
  Vanilla-Scented
  Granulated Sugar

Two 9-inch round break-apart cookies

Divide the dough into 2 discs. Place the discs between sheets of wax paper and roll out into a 9-inch circle. For each cookie, peel off the top sheet of wax paper, then invert the dough into the prepared tart pan. Press each round of dough evenly into the pan.

Bake the rounds on the middle-level rack of the oven for about 35 minutes, or until just firm to the touch.

Cool the cookies in the pans on 2 racks for 10 minutes. After 10 minutes, carefully set 1 tart pan on top of a small heatproof bowl (about 3 to 3½ inches in diameter), letting the outside frame drop to the countertop, then transfer the cookie (still on the metal bottom) back to the cooling rack. Repeat with the second tart pan. After about 20 minutes, carefully slide off each large cookie from the bottom of the tart pan onto the cooling rack, using a long, thin flexible palette knife. Invert each cookie, peel away the wax or parchment paper; invert again to right-side up.

Sprinkle the top of each cookie with ¾ tablespoon of the Vanilla-Scented Granulated Sugar. Cool the cookies for 1 hour, then store them in an airtight tin.

Apricot–Date Bars

FOR THE BROWN SUGAR
COOKIE LAYER:

1¼ cups *unsifted* all-
purpose flour

¼ teaspoon salt

8 tablespoons (1 stick)
unsalted butter,
softened at room
temperature

½ cup (firmly packed)
light brown sugar

1 teaspoon pure vanilla
extract

¼ teaspoon maple
extract

This is a two-layer bar cookie—a soft apricot and date spread bound with whole eggs and egg yolks covers a plain brown sugar cookie base. A plate of Apricot–Date Bars and one of Cinnamon–Cashew "Dunking" Cookies (page 102) would make a lovely midafternoon treat served with a pot of hot Earl Grey tea.

———❖❖❖———

Lightly butter and flour a 13 x 9 x 2-inch baking pan; set aside. Preheat the oven to 350 degrees.

For the brown sugar cookie layer, sift the flour and salt onto a sheet of wax paper.

Cream the butter in the large bowl of an electric mixer on moderate speed for 2 minutes. Beat in the brown sugar. Blend in the vanilla and maple extracts. On low speed (or by hand), blend in the sifted mixture in 2 additions, beating just until the particles of flour have been absorbed.

Press the cookie dough evenly on the bottom of the pre-pared pan. Bake the cookie layer on the middle-level rack of the oven for 15 to 20 minutes, or until firm to the touch. Remove from the oven and set aside on a cooling rack.

For the apricot–date spread, sift the cake flour, baking soda, salt, cinnamon and nutmeg into a large mixing bowl. Stir in the light brown sugar and granulated sugar. Beat in the egg and egg yolks. Stir in the preserves, dates and pecans. Spoon the topping evenly over the cookie base.

3 tablespoons *unsifted* cake flour

½ teaspoon baking soda

⅛ teaspoon salt

½ teaspoon ground cinnamon

¼ teaspoon freshly ground nutmeg

½ cup (firmly packed) light brown sugar

¼ cup granulated sugar

1 extra-large egg, at room temperature

2 extra-large egg yolks, at room temperature

¾ cup apricot preserves

1¼ cups chopped pitted dates

½ cup chopped pecans

---

36 bars

Bake on the middle-level rack of the oven for 25 minutes, or until the topping is set and firm to the touch.

Cool the baked cake in the pan on a rack until it reaches room temperature, about 2 hours. Cut the cake into 36 bars and store in an airtight tin.

Milk Chocolate–Almond Bars

½ pound (2 sticks) unsalted butter, cut into chunks

2 cups (about 12 ounces) chopped milk chocolate

1½ cups *unsifted* all-purpose flour

½ cup *unsifted* cake flour

½ teaspoon baking powder

¾ teaspoon salt

¾ cup chopped almonds

3 extra-large eggs, at room temperature

2 extra-large egg yolks, at room temperature

1¾ cups Vanilla-Scented Granulated Sugar (page 19)

2 teaspoons pure vanilla extract

1 teaspoon pure almond extract

½ teaspoon chocolate extract

36 bars

The mellow taste of milk chocolate and almonds, plus enough butter to enrich, makes this bar cookie distinctive. The batter is reinforced by vanilla-scented sugar and vanilla extract to complement the chocolate flavor.

As a summertime treat, serve the bars with glasses of iced tea or frosty goblets of iced coffee (add a cinnamon stick to each glass, if you like).

———❖❖❖———

Lightly butter and flour two 9-inch square baking pans. Line the bottom of each pan with a square of wax paper; set aside. Preheat the oven to 350 degrees.

Melt the butter and 1¼ cups milk chocolate in a heavy saucepan over very low heat; stir well, then set aside to cool.

Sift the all-purpose flour, cake flour, baking powder and salt onto a sheet of wax paper. Put the remaining ¾ cup chopped milk chocolate and almonds in a bowl and toss with 1 tablespoon of the sifted mixture.

Beat the eggs and egg yolks in a large mixing bowl. Beat in the sugar, vanilla, almond and chocolate extracts. Pour in the cooled chocolate–butter mixture and mix well. Stir in the sifted mixture in 2 additions, mixing just until the particles of flour have been absorbed. Fold in the floured chocolate and almonds.

Spoon the batter into the prepared pans, dividing it evenly between them.

Bake the bars on the middle-level rack of the oven for 30 to 35 minutes, or until set and each cake begins to pull away from the sides of the baking pan.

Cool the cakes in the pans on racks until they reach room temperature, about 2 hours. Invert each cake onto a second cooling rack, peel away the wax paper and invert again onto a cutting board.

Cut each cake into 18 bars and store them in an airtight tin.

Cinnamon–Cashew "Dunking" Cookies

2¼ cups *sifted* all-purpose flour

1 teaspoon baking powder

½ teaspoon salt

1 cup unsalted cashews, finely chopped

3 extra-large eggs, at room temperature

1 cup granulated sugar

1 cup vegetable oil

2 teaspoons pure vanilla extract

FOR SPRINKLING:

½ cup granulated sugar blended with 2 teaspoons ground cinnamon

About 36 cookies

These rectangular cookies are crisp and tender. The batter (made of oil, eggs, sugar, flour, leavening and cashews) is baked in old-fashioned ice cube trays—without the metal dividers. The trays hold just the right amount of batter, which bakes up into a soft, rounded loaf. The loaf is cut into ½-inch-thick slices, and the slices are doused with a haze of cinnamon sugar. Then you bake the slices in a low oven until they are quite crisp.

This recipe is from my mother's file. She used almonds instead of cashews, and the results are just as good. The idea for putting cashews in the batter comes from my friend and good cook, Mimi Davidson. This is one of my most requested cookie recipes, and it is so popular that I decided to work up some variations; they appear in this book as Chocolate Chip Rusks on page 106 and Layered Ginger Rusks on page 126. Cinnamon–Cashew "Dunking" Cookies keep magnificently in a cookie tin for several weeks—but only if you hide them.

❖❖❖

Lightly butter and flour two 11 x 4 x 1½-inch metal ice cube trays (with the divider inserts removed); set aside. Preheat the oven to 350 degrees.

Resift the flour with the baking powder and salt onto a sheet of wax paper. Put the cashews in a bowl and toss with 2 teaspoons of the sifted mixture.

Beat the eggs and sugar in the large bowl of an electric mixer on moderate speed for 2 minutes. Add the oil in a slow, steady stream, beating well. Increase the speed to moderately high and beat for 1 minute. Blend in the vanilla. On low speed (or by hand), add the sifted mixture in 2 additions, beating just until the particles of flour have been absorbed. By hand, stir in the cashews.

Spoon the batter into the prepared pans, dividing it evenly between them.

Bake on the middle-level rack of the oven for 30 minutes, or until well risen, firm to the touch and a wooden pick inserted into the center of each cake withdraws clean and dry.

Cool each cake in the pan on a rack for 3 to 5 minutes. Reduce the oven temperature to 250 degrees.

Invert each cake onto a second cooling rack and invert again to cool right side up. Let the cakes cool for 15 minutes.

Cut each cake into 18 slices with a sharp serrated knife. Arrange the slices on a large jelly roll pan (or large shallow baking pan). Sprinkle the slices evenly with half of the cinnamon sugar, turn the slices over and sprinkle with the remaining cinnamon sugar.

Bake the slices on the middle-level rack of the oven for about 20 to 30 minutes, to dry and crisp them. Turn the slices every 10 minutes with a pair of tongs. The slices should be quite firm—the tops should feel like toast instead of soft cake.

Transfer the cookies to cooling racks, using a wide spatula. Cool for 20 minutes. Store the cookies in an airtight tin.

Peach Squares

1¼ cups *unsifted* all-purpose flour

¼ cup *unsifted* cake flour

¼ teaspoon baking soda

¼ teaspoon baking powder

½ teaspoon salt

1 teaspoon ground cinnamon

¾ teaspoon freshly grated nutmeg

½ teaspoon ground ginger

½ teaspoon ground allspice

¼ teaspoon ground cloves

8 tablespoons (1 stick) unsalted butter, softened at room temperature

½ cup (firmly packed) light brown sugar

¼ cup granulated sugar

1 extra-large egg, at room temperature

2 extra-large egg yolks, at room temperature

These squares are chewy, spicy and chockablock full of dried peaches and pecans. I love them with a midafternoon cup of brewed decaffeinated coffee or mug of warm cider.

At my house, Peach Squares are served on a pale pink Depression-glass cookie plate, lined with heart-shaped paper doilies.

———❖❖❖———

Lightly butter and flour a 13 x 9 x 2-inch baking pan; set aside. Preheat the oven to 350 degrees.

Sift the all-purpose flour, cake flour, baking soda, baking powder, salt, cinnamon, nutmeg, ginger, allspice and cloves onto a sheet of wax paper.

Cream the butter in the large bowl of an electric mixer on moderate speed for 2 minutes. Add the brown sugar and beat for 2 minutes; add the granulated sugar and beat for one minute longer. Beat in the egg and the egg yolks, one at a time, blending well after each addition. Blend in the preserves. On low speed (or by hand), beat in the sifted mixture in 2 additions, beating just until the particles of flour have been absorbed. By hand, stir in the dried peaches, raisins and pecans.

Spoon the batter into the prepared pan, spreading it into an even layer with a spatula or flexible palette knife.

Bake the squares on the middle-level rack of the oven for 25 minutes, or until set and firm to the touch. (The cake will

½ cup peach preserves,
   blended with
   1 teaspoon pure
   vanilla extract
1 cup chopped dried
   peaches
¾ cup golden raisins
¾ cup chopped pecans

_____

24 squares

begin to pull away from the sides of the baking pan when done.)

Cool the cake in the pan on a rack until it reaches room temperature, about 2 hours. Cut the cake into 24 squares and store them in an airtight tin.

Chocolate Chip Rusks

2¼ cups *sifted* all-
purpose flour

1 teaspoon baking
powder

½ teaspoon salt

¾ cup miniature
semisweet chocolate
chips

3 extra-large eggs, at
room temperature

1 cup Vanilla-Scented
Granulated Sugar
(page 19)

1 cup vegetable oil

1½ teaspoons pure
vanilla extract

½ teaspoon chocolate
extract

FOR SPRINKLING:

⅓ cup Vanilla-Scented
Granulated Sugar

About 36 rusks

Chocolate Chip Rusks are the perfect cappuccino, hot chocolate or coffee cookie—they are sweet enough, tender-tex-
tured but firm, with enough chocolate to satisfy. Packed in
a checkered tin, they make a divine hostess gift.

———❖❖❖———

Lightly butter and flour two 11 x 4 x 1½-inch metal ice cube
trays (with the divider inserts removed); set aside. Preheat
the oven to 350 degrees.

Resift the flour with the baking powder and salt onto a
sheet of wax paper. Put the chocolate chips in a bowl and
toss with 2 teaspoons of the sifted mixture.

Beat the eggs and sugar in the large bowl of an electric
mixer for 2 minutes. Add the oil in a slow, steady stream,
beating well. Increase the speed to moderately high and
beat for 1 minute. Blend in the vanilla and chocolate extracts. On low speed (or by hand), add the sifted mixture in
2 additions, beating just until the particles of flour have
been absorbed. By hand, stir in the chocolate chips.

Spoon the batter into the prepared pans, dividing it
evenly between them.

Bake on the middle-level rack of the oven for 30 minutes,
or until well risen, firm to the touch and a wooden pick
inserted into the center of each cake withdraws clean and
dry.

Cool each cake in the pan on a rack for 2 to 3 minutes.
Reduce the oven temperature to 250 degrees.

Invert each cake onto a second cooling rack and invert again to cool right side up. Let the cakes cool for 15 minutes.

Cut each cake into 18 slices with a sharp serrated knife. Arrange the slices on a large jelly roll pan (or large shallow baking pan). Sprinkle the slices evenly with half of the sugar, turn the slices over and sprinkle with the remaining sugar.

Bake the slices on the middle-level rack of the oven for about 20 to 30 minutes, to dry and crisp them. Turn the slices over every 10 minutes with a pair of tongs. The slices should be quite firm—the tops should feel like toast instead of soft cake.

Transfer the cookies to cooling racks, using a wide spatula. Cool for 20 minutes. Store the cookies in an airtight tin.

"SNACKING" COOKIES

"SNACKING" COOKIES

—◆◆◆—

*F*ull of character and flavor, "snacking" cookies are those sweets made from nuts, oatmeal, dried fruit or preserves. Whether they are layered in tins or stacked in big jars, these cookies are good keepers; and I have found it wise to have a few dozen of them on hand for those who sneak into the kitchen at midnight for cookies and milk.

Brown Sugar–Fruit and Nut Mounds, Butterscotch–Granola Discs and Fruit Clusters are big and thick, bursting with a whole market list of ingredients: oatmeal, coconut, peanuts, cashews, sunflower seeds, bran, apricots, currants, raisins, figs and dates. These hearty cookies were made for pairing with goblets of cold milk or Hot Spiced Cider (page 133).

The Pecan Pie Squares and Layered Ginger Rusks are just sweet enough to accompany a pot of English Breakfast or Darjeeling tea, for a four o'clock tea-and-cookie break.

There are other recipes in this book for big-batch cookies that store well and are pleasing to have around for offering to children after school, or taking to the office and stashing in your desk drawer. My favorites are: Applesauce Pillows (page 40) and Apple Butter Cookies (page 80), Pear–Oatmeal Drops (page 44) and Oatmeal–Raisin Saucers (page 88), Pumpkin–Fig Mounds (page 46), Pumpkin–Spice Cookies (page 89) and Ginger Crisps (page 78).

Peanut Delights

2¾ cups *unsifted* all-
   purpose flour

¼ cup *unsifted* cake flour

¾ teaspoon baking soda

¾ teaspoon baking
   powder

¾ teaspoon salt

1½ teaspoons ground
   cinnamon

½ teaspoon ground
   ginger

½ teaspoon ground
   allspice

½ teaspoon freshly
   grated nutmeg

12 tablespoons
   (1½ sticks) unsalted
   butter, softened at
   room temperature

¾ cup shortening

¾ cup (firmly packed)
   light brown sugar

¾ cup superfine sugar

2 extra-large eggs, at
   room temperature

2 extra-large egg yolks,
   at room temperature

This big-batch recipe makes enough cookies to fill up a few cookie jars. These delights are full of the savor of smooth peanut butter and roasted peanuts. Spices and brown sugar complement the peanut flavor.

This is my mother's recipe for peanut butter cookies, one which I have changed slightly. I add a little light cream and molasses to the drop cookie dough, and replace part of the all-purpose flour with cake flour. Peanut Delights are always welcome at bake sales. If you are faced with baking many more dozens than this recipe turns out, know that great quantities of this dough can be made up and stored in the refrigerator for 2 to 3 days before baking. (And if your schedule is really frantic, turn these drop cookies into the slice-and-bake variety: Chill the dough thoroughly, then form into logs, 3 inches in diameter. Freeze the logs, then slice and bake as needed.)

❖❖❖

Lightly butter and flour 4 cookie sheets, or line the sheets with lengths of cooking parchment paper; set aside. Preheat the oven to 375 degrees.

Sift the all-purpose flour, cake flour, baking soda, baking powder, salt, cinnamon, ginger, allspice and nutmeg onto a sheet of wax paper.

Cream the butter and shortening in the large bowl of an electric mixer on moderate speed for 3 minutes. Add the brown sugar and beat for 1 minute; add the superfine sugar

1 teaspoon pure vanilla
  extract
3 tablespoons light
  molasses
3 tablespoons light
  cream, at room
  temperature
1⅓ cups smooth peanut
  butter
1¼ cups chopped lightly
  salted peanuts

About 48 cookies

and beat for 2 minutes. Add the eggs, one at a time, blending well after each addition; scrape down the sides of the mixing bowl frequently with a rubber spatula. Beat in the vanilla, molasses and cream. Beat in the peanut butter. On low speed (or by hand), blend in the sifted mixture in 2 additions, beating just until the particles of flour have been absorbed.

Drop the dough by level tablespoons onto the prepared cookie sheets, placing the mounds 1½ inches apart.

Bake the cookies, one sheet at a time, on the middle-level rack of the oven for 12 to 14 minutes, or until set and firm to the touch.

Transfer the cookies to cooling racks, using a wide spatula. Cool for 20 minutes. Store the cookies in an airtight tin.

Banana—
Oatmeal Pillows

2½ cups *sifted* all-purpose flour

1 cup *sifted* cake flour

1½ teaspoons baking soda

1 teaspoon baking powder

¾ teaspoon salt

2½ teaspoons ground cinnamon

1 teaspoon freshly grated nutmeg

½ teaspoon ground ginger

¼ teaspoon ground allspice

¼ teaspoon ground cloves

¾ cup shortening

4 tablespoons unsalted butter, softened at room temperature

1¼ cups (firmly packed) light brown sugar

¾ cup superfine sugar

2 extra-large eggs, at room temperature

This recipe is from my grandmother's cookie file: the pillows are soft, cakelike and full of the taste of ripe bananas and oatmeal. Over the years, I have modified the recipe to include lots more spices, flaked coconut, walnuts and a little molasses (some of the same ingredients that can be found in my favorite banana quick bread).

Banana—Oatmeal Pillows should be served with thick vanilla milk shakes or large cups of piping-hot coffee.

❖❖❖

Lightly butter and flour 4 cookie sheets, or line the sheets with lengths of cooking parchment paper; set aside. Preheat the oven to 375 degrees.

Resift the all-purpose flour and cake flour with the baking soda, baking powder, salt, cinnamon, nutmeg, ginger, allspice and cloves onto a sheet of wax paper.

Cream the shortening and butter in the large bowl of an electric mixer on moderate speed for 2 minutes. Add the brown sugar in 2 additions, beating for 1 minute after each portion is added. Add the superfine sugar and beat for 2 minutes. Add the eggs, one at a time, blending well after each addition. Beat in the egg yolks. Blend in the vanilla and almond extract; blend in the molasses and bananas. On low speed (or by hand), blend in the sifted mixture in 2 additions, beating just until the particles of flour have been absorbed. By hand, stir in the oatmeal, coconut and walnuts.

Drop the dough by rounded tablespoons onto the prepared cookie sheets, placing the mounds 1½ inches apart.

2 extra-large egg yolks,
    at room temperature

2 teaspoons pure vanilla
    extract

1 teaspoon pure almond
    extract

1 tablespoon light
    molasses

1½ cups mashed ripe
    bananas (about 3
    bananas)

2¾ cups quick-cooking
    oatmeal

¾ cup flaked coconut

¾ cup chopped walnuts

About 60 cookies

Bake the cookies one sheet at a time, on the middle-level rack of the oven for 13 to 14 minutes or until set and just firm to the touch.

Transfer the cookies to cooling racks, using a wide spatula. Cool for 20 minutes. Store the cookies in an airtight tin.

Brown Sugar—
Fruit and Nut
Mounds

1¾ cups *unsifted* all-
  purpose flour

¼ cup *unsifted* cake flour

1 teaspoon baking soda

1 teaspoon baking
  powder

1 teaspoon salt

1 teaspoon ground
  cinnamon

1 teaspoon freshly
  grated nutmeg

½ teaspoon ground
  allspice

½ pound (2 sticks)
  unsalted butter,
  softened at room
  temperature

1½ cups (firmly packed)
  brown sugar

½ cup superfine sugar

1 extra-large egg, at
  room temperature

2 extra-large egg yolks,
  at room temperature

2 teaspoons pure vanilla
  extract

Filled with dried fruit and oatmeal, these mounds are thick and hearty. Every year, around about the middle of December, my mother and I made these cookies in anticipation of the holidays. Weeks earlier, she'd order all the nuts, dried fruit and seeds from a supplier in California and store them in the pantry; with everything on hand, you knew that fruit cookies, fruitcakes and fruit-and-nut loaves were soon to be baked. Nowadays, the ingredients for these cookies are available at grocery stores, health food stores and most small markets.

Brown Sugar—Fruit and Nut Mounds can be made with almost any combination of dried fruit and nuts you can imagine. I am passing on our family recipe to you, and this list of substitutions: a mixture of filberts, Brazil nuts and almonds can replace the sunflower seeds, peanuts and cashews; currants or golden raisins can replace the dark seedless raisins; apricots or prunes can replace the peaches; and honey can replace the molasses.

❖❖❖

Lightly butter and flour 4 cookie sheets, or line the sheets with lengths of cooking parchment paper; set aside. Preheat the oven to 350 degrees.

Sift the all-purpose flour, cake flour, baking soda, baking powder, salt, cinnamon, nutmeg and allspice onto a sheet of wax paper.

Cream the butter in the large bowl of an electric mixer for 2 minutes. Add the brown sugar and beat for 2 minutes;

1 tablespoon light
  molasses

1 tablespoon light corn
  syrup

2¼ cups quick-cooking
  oatmeal

1 cup dark seedless
  raisins

1 cup flaked coconut

½ cup lightly salted
  cashews, chopped

½ cup lightly salted
  peanuts, chopped

¼ cup roasted unsalted
  sunflower seeds

1 cup chopped pitted
  dates

About 48 cookies

add the superfine sugar and beat for 1 minute. Beat in the egg and egg yolks, blending well. Beat in the vanilla, molasses and corn syrup. On low speed (or by hand), blend in the sifted mixture in 2 additions, beating just until the particles of flour have been absorbed. By hand, stir in the oatmeal, raisins, coconut, cashews, peanuts, sunflower seeds and dates.

Drop the dough by level tablespoons onto the prepared cookie sheets, placing the mounds 1½ inches apart.

Bake the cookies, one sheet at a time, on the middle-level rack of the oven for 10 to 12 minutes, or until just set and firm to the touch.

Transfer the cookies to cooling racks, using a wide spatula. Cool for 20 minutes. Store the cookies in an airtight tin.

Sour Cream–Molasses–Spice Rounds

2½ cups *unsifted* all-purpose flour

½ cup *unsifted* cake flour

1 teaspoon baking soda

½ teaspoon baking powder

1 teaspoon salt

2 teaspoons ground cinnamon

1½ teaspoons freshly grated nutmeg

½ teaspoon ground ginger

¼ teaspoon ground allspice

8 tablespoons (1 stick) unsalted butter, softened at room temperature

2 tablespoons shortening

½ cup (firmly packed) light brown sugar

¼ cup superfine sugar

⅓ cup molasses

¼ cup honey

These mounds are soft and golden brown, as good molasses cookies should be. The cinnamon and nutmeg, which I think of as sweet spices, balance out the assertive flavor of the molasses.

Cups of Hot Spiced Cider (page 133) or icy glasses of Real Lemonade (page 132) and a basket of Sour Cream Molasses–Spice Mounds would make a delightful afternoon snack.

———❖❖❖———

Lightly butter and flour 4 cookie sheets, or line the sheets with lengths of cooking parchment paper; set aside. Preheat the oven to 375 degrees.

Sift the all-purpose flour, cake flour, baking soda, baking powder, salt, cinnamon, nutmeg, ginger and allspice onto a sheet of wax paper.

Cream the butter and shortening in the large bowl of an electric mixer on moderate speed for 2 minutes. Add the brown sugar and beat for 1 minute; add the superfine sugar and beat for 1 minute. Blend in the molasses and honey (the mixture may look curdled, but it's okay). Beat in the egg and egg yolk. Blend in the vanilla extract. On low speed (or by hand), blend in the sifted mixture in 2 additions alternately with the sour cream in 1 addition, beginning and ending with the sifted mixture. By hand, stir in the raisins.

Drop the dough by level tablespoons onto the prepared cookie sheets, placing the mounds 1½–2 inches apart. Lightly sprinkle the cookies with the spiced sugar.

1 extra-large egg, at
  room temperature
1 extra-large egg yolk, at
  room temperature
1 teaspoon pure vanilla
  extract
¾ cup sour cream, at
  room temperature
¾ cup dark seedless
  raisins

FOR SPRINKLING:

½ cup granulated sugar
  blended with
  ¼ teaspoon ground
  cinnamon and
  ¼ teaspoon ground
  ginger

About 48 cookies

Bake the cookies, one sheet at a time, on the middle-level rack of the oven for 10 to 12 minutes, or until set and just firm to the touch.

Transfer the cookies to cooling racks, using a wide spatula. Cool for 20 minutes. Store the cookies in an airtight tin.

Fruit Clusters

¾ cup buttermilk, at
   room temperature

1 teaspoon baking soda

3 cups *sifted* all-purpose
   flour

¾ cup *sifted* cake flour

1 teaspoon baking
   powder

1 teaspoon salt

2½ teaspoons ground
   cinnamon

1½ teaspoons freshly
   grated nutmeg

1 teaspoon ground
   ginger

½ teaspoon ground
   allspice

½ pound (2 sticks)
   unsalted butter,
   softened at room
   temperature

1¼ cups (firmly packed)
   light brown sugar

¾ cup superfine sugar

3 extra-large eggs, at
   room temperature

1 extra-large egg yolk, at
   room temperature

Fruit clusters are soft, chewy and crammed full of apricots, dates, currants and figs; they will remind you of a good light fruitcake. The little kick of rum added to the cookie dough along with the vanilla extract intensifies the flavor of the fruit and nuts.

I serve a mound of Fruit Clusters from a pretty porcelain basket with cups of eggnog, mulled wine, Hot Spiced Cider (page 133) or coffee.

———❖❖❖———

Lightly butter and flour 4 cookie sheets, or line the sheets with lengths of cooking parchment paper; set aside. Preheat the oven to 350 degrees.

Pour the buttermilk into a bowl, stir in the baking soda and set aside.

Resift the all-purpose flour and cake flour with the baking powder, salt, cinnamon, nutmeg, ginger and allspice onto a sheet of wax paper.

Cream the butter in the large bowl of an electric mixer on moderate speed for 3 minutes. Add the brown sugar and beat for 2 minutes; add the superfine sugar and beat for 1 minute. Beat in the eggs, one at a time, blending well after each addition. Beat in the egg yolk. Blend in the vanilla and rum. On low speed (or by hand), blend in the sifted mixture in 3 additions alternately with the buttermilk in 2 additions, beginning and ending with the sifted mixture. By hand, stir in the apricots, dates, figs, currants, raisins, walnuts and pecans.

1 tablespoon pure
   vanilla extract

3 tablespoons light rum

1½ cups chopped glazed
   apricots

¾ cup chopped pitted
   dates

¾ cup chopped
   stemmed dried figs

½ cup currants

½ cup dark seedless
   raisins

1 cup chopped walnuts

½ cup chopped pecans

About 60 cookies

Drop the dough by level tablespoons onto the prepared cookie sheets, placing the mounds 2 inches apart.

Bake the cookies, one sheet at a time, on the middle-level rack of the oven for 15 minutes, or until golden, set and just firm to the touch.

Transfer the cookies to cooling racks, using a wide spatula. Cool for 20 minutes. Store the cookies in an airtight tin.

Butterscotch–Granola Discs

1¾ cups *unsifted* all-purpose flour

¼ cup *unsifted* cake flour

2 teaspoons baking powder

1½ teaspoons baking soda

¾ teaspoon salt

1 teaspoon ground cinnamon

¾ teaspoon freshly grated nutmeg

¼ teaspoon ground allspice

8 tablespoons (1 stick) unsalted butter, softened at room temperature

½ cup shortening

1¼ cups (firmly packed) light brown sugar

¼ cup superfine sugar

2 extra-large eggs, at room temperature

2 tablespoons light molasses

Making your very own "house blend" of granola is a quick and satisfying project. While no two mixtures ever come out the same, it's fun to mix and match the oats, bran, wheat germ, spices, nuts, fruit, seeds and sweeteners. Homemade granola makes a very good batch of cookies, but store-bought granola works well too. If you are using commercially produced granola and it lacks coconut or raisins, add about ⅓ cup raisins to this cookie dough, along with ¼ cup flaked coconut. Following this recipe is my own quirky recipe for granola, which I keep in a large wide-mouth apothecary jar on the kitchen counter.

Accompany a heaping plateful of Butterscotch–Granola Discs with a large pitcher of ice-cold milk.

————◈◈◈————

Lightly butter and flour 4 cookie sheets, or line the sheets with lengths of cooking parchment paper; set aside. Preheat the oven to 375 degrees.

Sift the all-purpose flour, cake flour, baking powder, baking soda, salt, cinnamon, nutmeg and allspice onto a sheet of wax paper.

Cream the butter and shortening in the large bowl of an electric mixer on moderate speed for 2 minutes. Add the brown sugar and beat for 2 minutes; add the superfine sugar and beat for a minute longer. Beat in the eggs, one at a time, blending well after each addition. Blend in the molasses, vanilla and maple extracts. On low speed (or by hand), blend in the sifted mixture in 2 additions, beating

2 teaspoons pure vanilla
  extract
1 teaspoon maple extract
1½ cups granola
  (homemade or store-
  bought)
1 cup butterscotch chips

About 48 cookies

just until the particles of flour have been absorbed. By hand,
stir in the granola and butterscotch chips.

Drop the dough by level tablespoons onto the prepared
cookie sheets, placing the mounds 1½ inches apart.

Bake the cookies, one sheet at a time, on the middle-level
rack of the oven for 12 to 14 minutes, or until set and just
firm to the touch.

Transfer the cookies to cooling racks, using a wide spatula. Cool for 20 minutes. Store the cookies in an airtight tin.

Homemade Granola

7 cups oats, quick-
cooking or old-
fashioned

1 cup bran

1 cup wheat germ

2 cups flaked coconut

1 cup unsalted sunflower
seeds

1 cup chopped walnuts

1 cup chopped pecans

1 teaspoon ground
cinnamon

¾ teaspoon freshly
grated nutmeg

1 cup pure maple syrup,
or to taste

1 tablespoon plus
1 teaspoon pure
vanilla extract

2 teaspoons maple
extract

1½ cups dark seedless
raisins

About 16½ cups

Full of what's good for you.

Lightly oil two 15 x 10 x 1-inch jelly roll pans; set aside. Preheat the oven to 275 degrees.

Combine the oatmeal, bran, wheat germ, coconut, sunflower seeds, walnuts, pecans, cinnamon and nutmeg in a large (8–10 quart) mixing bowl. Whisk together the maple syrup, vanilla and maple extracts; pour over the oat mixture and toss well.

Spread the granola evenly on the jelly roll pans, dividing the mixture between them. Bake the granola on the upper- and lower-third level racks of the oven for about 45 minutes, or until lightly toasted, stirring the mixture from time to time.

Cool the granola in the pans on a rack until room temperature, about 1½ hours. Crumble the granola into a large storage container, add the raisins and toss. Cover tightly and store at room temperature.

Pecan Pie Squares

1 cup *unsifted* all-purpose flour

⅓ cup *unsifted* cake flour

½ teaspoon baking soda

½ teaspoon baking powder

½ teaspoon salt

½ teaspoon ground cinnamon

½ teaspoon freshly grated nutmeg

¼ teaspoon ground allspice

1½ cup chopped pecans

12 tablespoons (1½ sticks) unsalted butter, melted and cooled

1½ cups (firmly packed) light brown sugar

3 tablespoons dark corn syrup

3 extra-large eggs, at room temperature

2 teaspoons pure vanilla extract

24 squares

These golden-colored squares are thick with chopped pecans, sweetened with brown sugar and corn syrup and enriched with butter. Serve them with a pot of hot tea (or pitcher of iced lemon tea), cups of spiced wine or a good bourbon-spiked eggnog.

Lightly butter and flour a 13 x 9 x 2-inch baking pan; set aside. Preheat the oven to 350 degrees.

Sift the all-purpose flour, cake flour, baking soda, baking powder, salt, cinnamon, nutmeg and allspice onto a sheet of wax paper. Put the pecans in a bowl and toss with 1 tablespoon of the sifted mixture.

Whisk the melted butter, brown sugar, corn syrup and eggs in a large mixing bowl, beating well. Blend in the vanilla. Stir in the sifted mixture in 2 additions, beating just until the particles of flour have been absorbed. Stir in the pecans.

Spoon the batter into the prepared pan, smoothing over the top with a spatula.

Bake on the middle-level rack of the oven for 30 to 35 minutes, or until set and firm to the touch (the cake will begin to pull away from the sides of the baking pan when done).

Cool the cake in the pan on a rack until it reaches room temperature, about 2 hours. Cut into 24 squares and store them in an airtight tin.

Layered Ginger Rusks

2¼ cups *sifted* all-
purpose flour

1 teaspoon baking
powder

½ teaspoon salt

¼ teaspoon ground
ginger

¾ cup roasted almonds,
finely chopped

3 extra-large eggs, at
room temperature

1 cup granulated sugar

1 cup vegetable oil

2 tablespoons freshly
squeezed orange juice

1 tablespoon freshly
grated orange peel

½ cup ginger preserves,
at room temperature

FOR SPRINKLING:

⅓ cup granulated sugar

About 36 rusks

Patterned after the luscious Cinnamon–Cashew "Dunking" Cookies on page 102, these rusks are flavored with ginger preserves, orange juice and grated orange rind.

For a splendid teatime treat, serve a basket of Layered Ginger Rusks with cups of hot orange or English Breakfast tea, or a pitcher of minted iced tea. For dessert, offer the rusks with poached pears, a toss of summer berries or homemade caramel ice cream.

———❖❖❖———

Lightly butter and flour two 11 x 4 x 1½-inch metal ice cube trays (with the divider inserts removed); set aside. Preheat the oven to 350 degrees.

Resift the flour with the baking powder, salt and ginger onto a sheet of wax paper.

Put the almonds in a bowl and toss with 2 teaspoons of the sifted flour mixture.

Beat the eggs and sugar in the large bowl of an electric mixer on moderate speed for 2 minutes. Add the oil in a slow, steady stream, beating well. Increase the speed to moderately high and beat for 1 minute. Beat in the orange juice and orange peel. On low speed (or by hand), add the sifted flour mixture in 2 additions, beating just until the particles of flour have been absorbed. By hand, stir in the almonds.

Divide the batter in half. Spoon *half* of 1 portion of batter into the prepared pans, dividing it evenly between them. Spoon ¼ cup preserves over the top of each pan of batter, leaving a ¾-inch border. Spoon the remaining portion of batter on top of the ginger layer, dividing it evenly between the 2 pans.

Bake on the middle-level rack of the oven for 30 minutes, or until well risen, firm to the touch and a wooden pick inserted into the center of each comes out clean and dry.

Cool the rusks in the pans on a rack for 3 to 5 minutes. Reduce the oven temperature to 250 degrees.

Invert each onto a second cooling rack and invert again to cool right side up. Let the cakes cool for 20 minutes.

Cut each cake into 18 slices with a sharp serrated knife. Arrange the slices on a large jelly roll pan (or large shallow baking pan). Sprinkle the slices evenly with half of the sugar; turn the slices over and sprinkle with the remaining sugar.

Bake the slices on the middle-level rack of the oven for 20 to 30 minutes, to dry and crisp them. Turn the slices every 10 minutes with a pair of tongs. The slices should be quite firm—the tops should feel like toast instead of soft cake.

Transfer the cookies to cooling racks, using a wide spatula. Cool for 20 minutes. Store the cookies in an airtight tin.

REFRESHMENTS
FOR A COUNTRY DAY

Wendy Wheeler

REFRESHMENTS FOR A COUNTRY DAY

❖❖❖

*R*eal Lemonade, Hot Spiced Cider and Summer Fruit Medley are all splendid beverages to serve alongside a plate of just-baked cookies. The lemonade and the mixed fruit drink, a pair of fresh and lively thirst quenchers, taste mighty good with many of the cookies in this book, especially the Vanilla Melt-a-Ways (page 32), Sugar Cookie Hearts (page 84), Double Vanilla "Dog Bones" (page 54), Ginger Crisps (page 78), Lemon Butter Balls (page 58) or Black Walnut Butter Drops (page 94). A pitcher of warm cider is a heavenly match for a basket of Applesauce Pillows (page 40), Pumpkin–Fig Mounds (page 46), Maple Bars (page 52), Apple Butter Cookies (page 80), Apricot–Date Bars (page 98) or Oatmeal–Raisin Saucers (page 88). On a snowy weekend afternoon, offer mugs of cider and a tin of fresh cookies to neighbors; on a hot and balmy summer day, present tall glasses of lemonade with a dish of buttery cookies to friends and family after an outing to the pool or farmer's market.

Real Lemonade

FOR THE LEMON SYRUP:

2 cups water

2⅔ cups granulated
sugar

3 cups freshly squeezed
lemon juice (about
16 lemons)

TO FINISH:

About 4½ cups ice-cold
water (more or less, to
taste)

Thin slices of lemon
(optional)

Sprigs of fresh mint
(optional)

*About 8 cups, enough for
12 tall glasses*

With a sweet-tart taste, fresh lemonade is perfect for washing down a few cookies—or a slice of cake or wedge of pie. The base of this cooling drink is made up of a sugar syrup into which you pour freshly squeezed lemon juice. For serving, simply add several cupfuls of ice cold water to dilute the syrup; the lemon-enhanced syrup can be made several days in advance and kept in the refrigerator in a tightly sealed container. This recipe also turns out a sprightly batch of limeade if you substitute the same amount of lime juice for the lemon juice.

———❖❖❖———

Place the water and sugar in a medium-size stainless steel saucepan; cover and set over low heat. Cook slowly until every last granule of sugar has dissolved. Uncover the saucepan, raise the heat to moderately high and bring the liquid to a boil. Boil 5 minutes. Cool. Stir the lemon juice into the sugar syrup. (The syrup can be prepared up to this point, stored in a tightly sealed container and refrigerated for 5 to 7 days.)

To serve the lemonade, add most of the water (about 3½ cups) to the lemon syrup. Add the rest of the water, a little at a time, tasting as you go: the lemonade should be nicely balanced. If the drink is too heavy on the syrup, just add a little more water.

Pour the lemonade into tall glasses that have been filled with ice. Tuck a mint sprig into the glass to one side, and enjoy.

Hot Spiced Cider

6 cups fresh apple cider

¼ cup pure maple syrup
(more or less, to taste)

2 cinnamon sticks

6 whole cloves

6 whole allspice berries

6 strips orange peel

6 strips lemon peel

---

*About 6 cups, enough for
6 large mugs*

This is a comforting concoction that's far from fussy: It is unfiltered cider, sweetened with maple syrup, charged with spices and warmed to bring out all the pleasing aromas and flavors.

———❖❖❖———

Pour the apple cider and maple syrup into a large stainless steel saucepan. Place the cinnamon sticks, cloves, allspice berries, orange peel and lemon peel in the center of a washed square of cheesecloth; fold up the sides of the cheesecloth to enclose the spices in a bundle, then tie it up with a length of kitchen string. Drop the spice bundle into the cider mixture. Place the saucepan over moderate heat for 5 to 10 minutes, or until the cider is very hot but not boiling.

Remove the cider from the heat. Discard the spice bundle. Ladle the cider into big cups or mugs, adding a fresh cinnamon stick to each serving, if you like.

Summer Fruit
Medley

2 cups freshly squeezed
  grapefruit juice,
  chilled

1½ cups guava juice,
  chilled

1 cup peach nectar,
  chilled

1 cup pear nectar,
  chilled

1 cup freshly squeezed
  orange juice, chilled

⅓ cup fresh fruit syrup
  (homemade or store-
  bought)

2 tablespoons freshly
  squeezed lime juice

⅔ cup club soda, chilled

*About 7½ cups, enough for
6 tall glasses*

A blend of fruit juices, lightly sweetened with fresh fruit syrup and served in pretty glass tumblers is a good drink to have on hand during summer's sun-drenched days. A few splashes of light rum can be stirred into each drink, if the spirit moves you.

———❖❖❖———

Combine the grapefruit juice, guava juice, peach nectar, pear nectar, orange juice, fruit syrup and lime juice in a large pitcher. Stir in the club soda.

Pour the fruit medley into large ice-filled glasses and serve.

Note: Fruit syrups are wonderful to have on hand for adding to summer drinks, fruit salads and ice cream. The method for making a whole range of the syrups is outlined on pages 37 and 38 of *Country Pies,* one of the companion volumes to this book.

THE COUNTRY
COOKIE
EXCHANGE

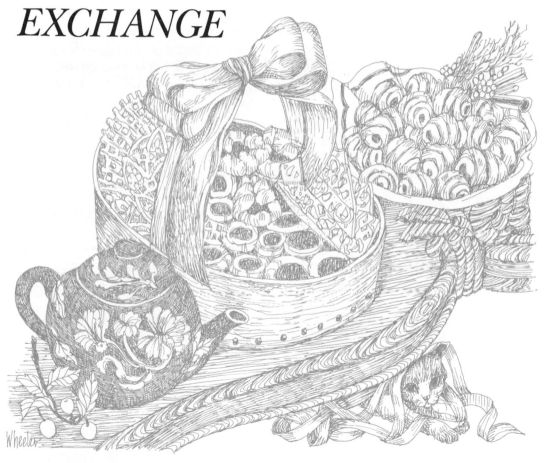

During the winter holidays when everyone loves to bake and have plenty of cookies squirreled away in tins, it's fun to organize an informal gathering to swap cookies and recipes. Participating in such an exchange is a good way to sample lots of baked things and take home masses of cookies besides.

As the host or hostess, invite twelve of the best cooks you know to take part in the exchange. Ask each person to send you his or her three favorite cookie recipes, then select one recipe from each submission, making sure that many flavors and textures are represented. Assign each cook one of his or her own recipes, and tell everyone to prepare twelve dozen cookies (or more, if you like). Along with the load of cookies, remind every baker to bring copies of the recipe and big containers for holding all the cookies they'll be taking home.

On the day of the swap, clear a large table. Set out packages of plastic bags, boxes of wax paper, twist ties and cellophane wrap.

Arrange a big pot of coffee or tea or eggnog on a sideboard to accompany the cookies you'll be sampling.

Ask each baker to set out his or her batch of cookies on the table and parcel them out into bags or boxes. The table, holding a mountain of cookies, will remind you of Santa's workshop. And the aroma of spices, butter, chocolate, nuts and fruit is a festive reminder of the days to come.

Country Cookies that Use "Goods on Hand" (Basic Dairy and Pantry Staples)

⋄⋄⋄

Country Cookies that Use Fresh or Dried Fruit

———— ◈◈◈ ————

Keeping Cookies

— ❖❖❖ —

Index

H

L

M

N

O

P

R

S

T

V

W

Have BETTER HOMES AND GARDENS® magazine
delivered to your door. For information, write to:
MR. ROBERT AUSTIN
P.O. BOX 4536
DES MOINES, IA 50336